SPITFIRE
POSTSCRIPT

by   C.R. RUSSELL

Published by the Author
12 Broomfield Drive, Alderholt,
Fordingbridge, Hampshire. SP6 3HY.
Typeset and printed by
REPROPRINT
Alderholt Parade, Alderholt,
Fordingbridge, Hampshire. SP6 3AA.

This book is dedicated in gratitude to

my wife

PATRICIA

and especially in recognition for

all the years of care she has

devoted to me.

ACKNOWLEDGEMENTS

My thanks to all those who took the time and trouble to write to me about their experiences and I trust they will understand when I say that they were too numerous for me to mention individually. I trust also that those whose contributions I have been unable to include will accept that their efforts were only omitted to avoid repetition. There is one exception that I must make which any reader will understand and that is the great contribution that Denis Webb has made with his accounts of the activities that took place during those eventful years and which but for his generosity may never have seen the light of day.

My thanks must also go to the many sources of photographs that became available to me which included Dr. Mark Nicholls of Cambridge University Library, Brian Wexham of Vickers Ltd., John Vasco, Stanley Brown, Frank Hamblin, Denis Webb, the Southern Evening Echo and Lawrence Cummins, Editor and Director of the Newbury Weekly News Group.

Contents

SELECTED BIBLIOGRAPHY

Against All Odds by Lex McAuley
A R P Reports. Southampton City Archives.
Aeroplane Monthly magazine.
Battle over Britain by Frank Mason.
Bombsights over Britain by John Vasco.
Beaverbrook by Anne Chisholm and Michael Davies.
Der Adler. German Air Force magazines.
Flight magazines.
Finest Hour by Martin Gilbert.
Flying Magazine. A prewar aeronautical magazine.
Spitfire - A Test Pilot's Story by Jeffrey Quill.
Spitfire - The History by Morgan and Shacklady.
Southampton at War by Anthony Kemp.
The Spitfire Story by Alfred Price.
The Southampton Evening Echo.
The Birmingham Post and Mail newspapers.
The Second World War, Vol. 2, by Winston Churchill.
The Southampton Blitz by Tony Brode.
The Right of the Line by John Terraine.
Blitz - Then and Now. Volume 2.
Luftwaffe Encore by Ken Wakefield.
A Grain of Sand by F.C. Shelley.

Introduction

Many thousands of words have been written over the course of the past fifty-five years on the subject of the Supermarine Spitfire. Most, quite rightly, praise the inspired genius of R.J. Mitchell and the design team that he led, whilst others, mainly test pilots and fighter pilots, attest faithfully to its flying and fighting capabilities which were to prove so decisive when the shock of war assailed our homeland, and later many other homelands all across the world.

However, much less has been said, or is known, about the production engineers, supervisors, the skilled and unskilled tradesmen, and the women and girls workers, who played their parts, sometimes in situations fraught with danger, in the manufacturing of the sleek and deadly fighter aircraft that was to become a household name and still evokes emotions and interest so many years later.

It was my good fortune to be employed by Vickers-Supermarine at their Woolston, Southampton, works just four days after the Spitfire prototype made its maiden flight in the hands of Mutt Summers, Vickers Chief Test Pilot, on March 5th 1936 from Eastleigh aerodrome. No-one at that time had any inkling of the contribution the aircraft would have on practically all our lives, and I now count it a privilege to have served my next eleven years as an apprentice and skilled tradesman with most of those years being dominated by the Spitfire and later on, the Seafire. It is those years that I propose to deal with in this form of a postscript, discounting the subsequent two periods when I rejoined the company in middle management positions, other than to draw on, the additional information, and colleagues, obtained during those extra years, and hopefully give recognition to the categories enumerated above that have, in my opinion, not received their due, whilst at the same time taking this opportunity to redress some of the stories that are extant today which, unless clarified or refuted, might be taken as factual and mislead future generations of Spitfire buffs. Way back in 1985 I was fortunate enough to have accepted for publishing my own autobiographical account of all my time with Supermarines under its title 'Spitfire Odyssey' which, although now out of print, can still be obtained through the national public lending library service. Following that book's release I received many letters from all over the world, many from old colleagues and many also from people I did not even know. One of the 'unknowns' was kind enough to write "Thank you for telling our story" which I thought rather nice and highlighted the fact that until then it appears that no one had written an account of what the Spitfire saga meant to the thousands who had participated in its manufacture from the 'shop-floor' viewpoint. From what they wrote and said it was obvious that they wished I had gone further than just my personal story, and in particular had taken steps to amend some of the wilder accounts that have appeared since and mostly emanate from people who were not present at the time, or not involved with the subject close enough to form a reasonable view, or the product of those who are supposed to be historians. There are, of course, the genuine mistakes - memory has a nasty habit of playing tricks, especially as one gets older - and there are also the printing errors; but that aside there is no doubt in my mind that it is advisable to be wary when one is presented with 'historically eminent persons' accounts which are based solely on 'official' records. The incident of the Hitler Diaries reminds us all that even the most exalted of 'historians' can make dreadful blunders, and more recently we have one, so called, 'historian' who would have us believe that the holocaust in the Nazi concentration camps is a figment of our imagination or propaganda disseminated by the Jewish community.

Once I had made it known that I was prepared to comply with my correspondent's suggestion the information poured in and I began the sifting and research required to give, as best I can, this postscript, as I have chosen to call it, on the production of the Spitfire, and also some of the peripheral events that surrounded its manufacture.

During my research I was introduced to the activities of one particular German Luftwaffe Group who had a very direct bearing on the subject matter so I have included a chapter about them, because although they were 'the enemy' with the passage of time saner counsels have prevailed and the short, and terrible cost of their efforts are worth recording.

At the conclusion of my tale I shall be able to relate something that gave me great personal pleasure and will provide a fitting end on a happier note.

Chapter one - The Beginning

When, as a mid-teenager, I walked first into the workshops of the Supermarine's Woolston Works it was buzzing with the activities associated with the flying boat construction with which they were heavily engaged. I was taken by the gate warden to the time office of the hull shop as it was known and allocated the employee number K.175. The 'K' I later learned indicated that this was the shop where the Keels of the flying boat hulls were laid as the first step to their build. It was some little time, much later on that first day, before I began to sense, more than hear or understand, that various little groups of men and lads of my own age were saying quite excitedly "that the fighter had flown last Thursday".

When I had a further couple of days acclimatisation to the unaccustomed noise of the workshop and could gradually begin to hear what other people were saying when they spoke to me I ventured an enquiry about the 'fighter'. In that manner I became aware that the Spitfire prototype had been built at the eastern end of the shop I was in, had successfully made its first flight at Eastleigh, and that was about all.

The events at Eastleigh that followed have been chronicled many times elsewhere in books and on screens and it is sufficient for me to say no more than that after a few minor modifications and further test flights the prototype duly flew over the Woolston Works shortly afterwards at lunch time, and the word was passed around so that those employees interested could see it. I went out onto the slipway and saw it, as did many others, but until the production order affected K shop over a year later, I was not involved.

We now know that an intense effort was being made at Eastleigh to have the Prototype prepared to undergo its essential testing by the Royal Air Force's Experimental Aircraft centre at Martlesham Heath prior to its acceptance as suitable for R.A.F. pilots to fly and thus lead to the placing of a production order. We know as well, that there was a certain haste in these matters as the government had ordered rearming against the growing threat from Hitler's Germany.

We know too, that special arrangements were made to facilitate the Spitfire's clearance at Martlesham so that instructions could be given to Vickers to proceed with all speed with an order for 310 aircraft.

Having spent my latter years in the aircraft industry in production management executive positions I can well appreciate the consternation that an order of this magnitude (most of their previous orders for flying boats seldom exceeded 30, and often less) caused to the design and production staffs. At the time when the prototype was being built at Woolston it was a 'one off', made in the least expensive manner possible, with all the speed that could be engendered, and so far as the location allowed, in secret. The design drawings would most often not be as comprehensive as production drawings for general issue would need to be, and no doubt occasionally a sketch would be sufficient information for work to be done by hand or very primitive tooling. To productionise the drawings meant that they all had to be drawn afresh, traced onto the printing media, (at the time the D.O. only had two young lady tracers) and as if that was not enough, the R.A.F. assessment of the aircraft at Martlesham was continually feeding back the changes they thought necessary to improve the product for their use.

Although the Company had received an order dated 3rd June 1936 for the 310 aircraft it had not been supplied with the Specification details that arose from the Martlesham testing assessments until some eight weeks later, one of which was to cause a measure of delay that affected the subsequent delivery promises, namely the requirement to stiffen up the wing leading edges from 16 gauge alloy sheet to 14 gauge to increase the strength of the leading edge torsion box which was crucial to Mitchell's 'thin wing' design. This change, and many other less serious alterations had to be incorporated into the new production drawings and naturally had an effect on the tooling that would be required.

It should, of course, not be forgotten that in the period between the prototype's maiden flight and the first production aircraft's leap into the air in 1938 that R.J. Mitchell had died at the relatively young age of 42, thus depriving the industry and the country of a creative genius at a time when he was probably needed most. Joe Smith, who had been Mitchell's Design Office Chief

The Supermarine Works at Woolston in the early 20's. Mitchell's office the rectangular window behind and to left of slipway. Source Vickers.

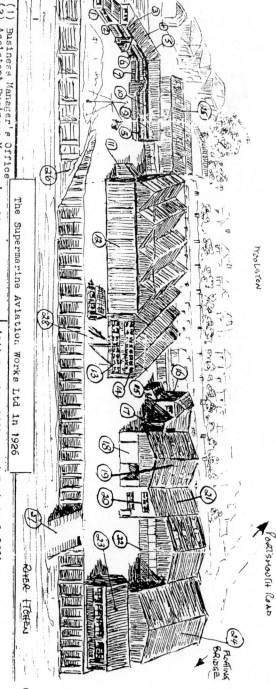

(1) Business Manager's Office.
(2) Assistant Business Manager's office.
(3) Board Room.
(4) Chief Accountant and Cashier's Offices
(5) Management Canteen.
(6) Publicity Office.
(7) Test Pilot's Office.
(8) Telephone Exchange and Enquiries.
(9) Wages Office.
(10) Costing Office.
(11) Tank Cleaning Hut.
(12) Erecting Shop and Wooden Hull Shop.Built 1926.
(13) Machine Shop. Built around 1924 "
(14) Fitting Shop. " "
(15) Time Clerks Hut. " "
(16) Welfare Office and Mess Room.
(17) Boiler House.
(18) Wing Shop. Built around 1916.
(19) Modification Drawing Office over Wing Shop.
(20) R.J.Mitchell's Office.

The Supermarine Aviation Works Ltd in 1926

(21) Drawing Office and Technical Offices.
(22) Dope Shop and Sheet Metal Shop.
(23) Heat Treatments,Stove Enamelling,Lavatories.This was one of the earliest buildings.
(24) Metal Hull Shop. Partly built before 1919.
(25) Woodmill and Carpenters Snop.
(26) Remains of old Yacht Slipway.
(27) Flying Boat Slipway.
(28) Shearlegs.

NOTE.

The site of the Factory had originally been a Yacht Basin with several yacht slipways. The General Office block (1) to (10) had originally been a Yacht Chandlers stores and Sail Loft. Built partly of brick with a corrugated iron roof it had two floors and access to the offices was by external verandas and external but covered stairways. It was probably built around 1916.

Portsmouth Road

River Itchen

Floating Bridge (34)

Draughtsman took over the Chief Designer's position and ably supported by the team that Mitchell had gathered around him, plus the new men and women that arrived to enlarge what to me had seemed to be a ridiculously small design team originally, carried through all the modifications that arose in the years ahead to keep the Spitfire as the number one British single seater fighter until the coming war's end. That they coped, and coped magnificently, with all the fluctuating circumstances, is to the Design Department's eternal credit.

But all this is only the backdrop to the production story that I wish to relate.

The man primarily responsible for all the production activities at Supermarine was Trevor Westbrook. He had been appointed General Manager when Vickers bought out the controlling interest in the Company in 1928 and was responsible to Vickers Director of Aircraft Production, Sir Robert McLean at Weybridge. Weybridge trained and totally dedicated to his work, he knew what he wanted and drove hard to ensure he got it. Never one for small talk, neither did he suffer fools gladly, he was, as I know by personal experience, firm and fair, but God help you if you tried to mislead him. If he had a fault, it was that he was a 'hustler' - he was into everything no matter where you were, or what you were doing, there was always the chance that this rapidly moving man with his stern, aggressive good looks might descend from nowhere and ask the most damned awkward question. However, in the June of 1936 he was the right man in the right place. With a delivery promise, given by Sir Robert McLean in his discussions with the Air Ministry, "that provided the production order is signed by May 1st 1936 the firm would be able to start production deliveries in September 1937 and with a production rate of 5 per week it should be possible to complete 360 to 380 aircraft by 31st March 1939." Westbrook must have known that he faced a major challenge, especially as the small Woolston works was already crammed with orders for Australian Seagull's and R.A.F. Walrus amphibians (both these were virtually identical but the Australians had ordered and named their aircraft first.) The last of the Scapa flying boats and just about to commence an order for 17 Stranraer flying boats.

It was immediately obvious to Westbrook, as it had been to the visiting representatives from the Air Ministry during their site visits to see and discuss the prototype, that there was not enough floor space and that it would have to be necessary to employ subcontractors. Board approval was given to enlarge the Woolston site as much as possible, but there were limits as the whole site was contained within a pile-driven area with no further land to extend on. However, a large proportion of the apron above the slipway was successfully enclosed and became integral to the main workshops, whilst at the northern end where the clearance of gatewarden's post, the cycle racks for employees, and what acted as the transport department, made sufficient room to build a new block to house the design office and various other departments. All this could take another year and time was pressing.

Although it must have been galling to Sir Robert McLean to lose the benefits he thought they were entitled to in financial terms almost two thirds of the aircraft had to be subcontracted.

The Woolston factory retained the build of the main fuselage, which by this time it had been decided required a 'transport joint' at the frame 19 position, and most fortunately the wing's torsion box.

Fortunately also, none of the modifications the Ministry required had affected the main 'pick-up points' that are essential to know for the manufacture of main jigs. The Tool Design Office under Jack Knowles speedily issued the drawings that enabled the Production Manager, Jim Butler, to proceed with the construction of the jig framework made from 'H' iron section and set in hand the details that would hold the main wing attachment fitting at frame five, the rear spar attachment further back, and the heavy plate that would provide the location for the forward half of the joint frame at the rear of the fuselage where the empennage assembly would have to fit. Contour plates shaped to clear, but adhere to, the fuselage's centre line top and bottom shape were made from 1/2 inch plate and welded to them were pick-up locations for each of the frames. These plates were held by castings that were bolted to the main jig frame but were capable of being moved up and down when the plating operations took place or the completed fuselage was ready for removal from the jig.

The side of K shop adjacent to the wing shop was cleared gradually and the first fuselage jig was erected from drawing dimensions only with 'stick-micrometers', theodolite, and a central datum of tensioned piano wire for use with a plumb-bob. Everything was checked and re-checked by the works Inspectors, and the A.I.D. for the Ministry, against the drawing dimensions. Contours were obtained from the Mould Loft scrieve boards produced under the direction of Don Snooks.

Anyone who has worked in aircraft manufacturing when it is engaged in getting a new type into production will understand when I say that gradually, from the seeming chaotic, the tender shoots of order and purpose slowly emerge.

With Production aircraft it is essential that interchangeability and repeatability is established from the start and to these ends a second fuselage jig was built in the same time-consuming way as the first, so that when crosschecked the product from one jig would fit into the other and vice-versa. Frame 5 was the main frame for the fuselage as it embodied the main spar wing attachments, the engine mounting pick-up points as well as the bottom and centre fuselage longeron attachment fittings. Once the first frame 5 became available it was tried in both jigs to ensure that the wing attachment fittings were correct. Once this was shown as satisfactory the frame was left in the second jig whilst the first jig was passed over to the tool-makers for them to build two interchangeability checking 'male' four inch tubular steel, jigs that simulated a completed fuselage and provided an inspection or checking media of all the relevant pick-up points. Meanwhile the second jig continued with the build of the fuselage proper as the supply of frames and longerons began to trickle from our own shops and some subcontractors, so that by the time the 'interchangeability' tubular jig was available a crosscheck could be made by placing it in the second jig after the fuselage structure (now rivetted) was removed, and trying the rivetted structure in the first jig. There were probably minor adjustments necessary but nothing that the odd piece of shimming could not cure, and once the Inspectors for the Company and the Ministry had approved both jigs were cleared for production.

The rivetted structure was returned to the second jig and its skinning operations begun, the first jig was retained to make the second Interchange jig, and the first interchange jig was used to set the jig points on the third of the jigs in the row that crept slowly down that one side of the workshop. The second interchange jig, once completed, was crated and sent away to Ministry storage as the 'master'.

Whilst all this activity had been going on a similar performance was taking place just a few feet away in 'P' shop, where the leading edge torsion box was to be built in an area underneath the planning offices which had been cleared of flying boat aerofoil structures that had been assembled there previously prior to their doping and fabricing operations.

The progress of this leading edge was to prove both troublesome and, later on, most fortuitous. At first there were the delays brought about by the leading edge stiffening that necessitated alterations to the big press tools at the subcontractors, and a supply of the main spar boxed sections had to be put on a production basis at their suppliers.

Supermarines, at that time, had no really satisfactory press tool facilities. The biggest press tool was only a 60 ton one with a very modest platen bed of roughly 18" x 12", no rubber press, no brake press, in fact nothing that was capable of producing 'in house', the wing leading edge skins, the wing main spar sections, or even the engine's top cowling panel. They had for years relied on the skills of, very often, individual specialist craftsmen to achieve the successes associated with the Schneider Trophy and subsequent metal flying boats designed by R. J. Mitchell. It is to their eternal credit that they did so well. In its initial stages the weight of the Spitfire production fell on the tradesmen in the tool room, machine shop, detail fittings shop, the tank shop and as I have mentioned, the hull and wing shops. Eventually it spread to encompass the whole factory.

In the race to obtain the extra space required, in addition to the extensions already mentioned at the Woolston works, the smaller site opposite the main gate in Hazel Road was extended considerably to enlarge the Woodwork and Dope shops, as well as creating an air-raid control centre and a casualty clearing area. The portents were ominous!

Supermarines Woolston Works after the new building and extensions. Source Vickers.

A Walrus hull being transported to the Itchen Works. Note the overhead walkway leading from the main Woolston Works into the new Woodwork, Paint and Dope shops. Source D. Webb.

Inside the Itchen Works 1939. Note continuing flying boat build in background. Vickers.

Once the new design office block was built it was connected by a covered walkway into what was then the Tank shop balcony, and later this walkway was extended to cross over Hazel Road and lead directly into the Dope shop. Further along Hazel Road a small two storey building was erected, its upper floor exclusively for the Mould Loft and underneath the cycle storage racks for the employees which had been earlier located where the new design block was established.

Even further along the riverside, beyond where Hazel Road petered out into a rough, unmade, gravel road a large patch of land between Taggart's wood storage sheds and the entrance to Whites Shipyard a brand new main assembly shop was erected and became known as the Itchen Works.

Equally important, as the frenzied activity at the Southampton end of the business, the vital importance of locating and engaging subcontractors and establishing liaison channels was being pursued with all the pressure Trevor Westbrook could apply. There can be little doubt now that his particular brand of drive (one is tempted to say bullying) did much to instil the urgency attached to the task felt necessary in Government circles. The General

Itchen Works Assembly line for Spitfire fuselages prior to their dispatch to Eastleigh. Production numbers can be seen on the front bulkheads. Vickers.

Aircraft Co and Pobjoy Motors Ltd were allocated the wing build, J Samuel White at Cowes the fuselage frames, Westland Aircraft at Yeovil, and G Beaten, undertook the wing ribs, Folland Aircraft at Hamble (the nearest to the parent design offices) were entrusted with the rear fuselage empennage, whilst the two suppliers of most crucial items in the wing leading edge box, the extruded square box-within-box main spars were made by British Aluminium from the material Hiduminium, and the top and bottom, port and starboard, leading edge skins came from the Pressed Steel Co.

Having had a hand in initiating most of the foregoing in his role as General Manager, Trevor Westbrook was rather suddenly called back to Vickers main Weybridge Works where Sir Robert McLean considered his presence more essential in producing the new Wellington Bombers.

He formally left us on December 31st 1936, having been at Supermarines since the Vickers takeover in 1928 during which time he had established himself as the driving force in the production side of the Schneider Trophy seaplanes that ultimately won the trophy outright, and practically all the metal flying boats since Supermarines changed over from wooden materials to metal. To be honest, I thought he was with us longer than that, it certainly seemed longer to me, but as one of my older colleagues has remarked "time goes slower when you are in your teens", but the year end change has been substantiated for me by privately published books on the subject of Vickers history.

His place was filled as general Manager by Mr H. Pratt, who, I understand, had been associated with Barnes-Wallis during Vickers airship building ventures. One immediate benefit from this change was that Mr. Pratt settled himself in to doing the administration functions and so allowed Wilfred Elliot to assert himself as the Works Manager which had rather been overshadowed by the more thrusting Westbrook.

Nowhere have I seen the due regard paid to Wilfred Elliot that was, and still is, his for the manner in which he carried out the heavy burdens that were his lot over the following ten years.

Elliot's association with Supermarine went back a long way and he was Works Manager before Vickers took over in 1928 and some of my older colleagues recall him in that position prior to 1926 when they commenced working there.

Among the many letters I received after the publication of Spitfire Odyssey was one from Denis Webb who had served as personal assistant - or 'general dogsbody' as he puts it himself - to both Westbrook and Elliot. As he too was engaged in writing the memories of his, much longer, years than mine at Supermarine, this led to a considerable amount of letters between us as he knew me at Hursley Park and was aware that I could assist him with information in areas where he had not been involved, whilst he could give me a mass of information that I was unaware, or had only little knowledge, which would be to our mutual benefit. Fortunately we both agreed that either of us could use any of each others material, with the rider that the responsibility for any libel litigation was carried by whoever published it.

I intend to draw extensively on this source because, knowing the man, the positions he held, I can rely - with very few exceptions - that his accounts are trustworthy.

Denis Webb joined Supermarine in 1926 and was fortunate in the fact that his father was in a position to pay the premium then required for him to have a Grade 'A' Apprenticeship. He did three years serving in various trade categories in the workshops, then spells in the Progress, Wages and Costing, Design, Inspection (stamp no. 6S 28), Contracts, and ending up in the Business Manager's office where it looked like he would become a Commercial assistant to Mr. Marsh-Hunn the then Business Manager.

However, he was spotted by Westbrook who wanted someone to reorganise the Finished Part Stores, which I gather was in something of a mess. That he did this quite successfully I can personally vouch for because it was there I first ran across him as Finished Part Store Manager when I was searching for some parts that the men I was working for (as their boy) had sent me to fetch. However, he was not there long as he was required by Westbrook for various jobs to speed production.

When Westbrook left, Elliot retained his services for the same personal assistant role which he held until Elliot wanted him for other important jobs that arose, particularly after war was declared, and which I think will best be dealt with in the chronology of this narrative.

Wilfred Elliot was almost the exact opposite to Westbrook in the way he dealt with the workshops. He had Arthur Nelson as Superintendent - a term that was to change its ranking in future years, but at that time meant he was in charge of all the Foremen - and by and large he dealt through Nelson to those Foremen, not pouncing out of the blue as Westbrook was prone to do, and those Foremen were able to operate in a much better manner when they felt that they were truly in charge of their individual workshops and able to liaise personally, or via their shop Progress Chaser, when there were the inevitable inter-shop queries, but still able to go to Nelson if the difficulties were too great for them to deal with, who in turn could refer to Elliot for a decision if necessary. As an illustration of this, my own foreman, William Heaver, was able to get me raised from my original engagement as a 'handy lad' to an indentured apprenticeship, something I don't think he would have broached with Westbrook. That move in status changed the remainder of my own life as I had been offered an office job which would have turned out to be a disastrous blind alley.

Within Elliot's overall control now came the Production Offices the Planning, Estimating, and Rate fixing looked after by James Butler, with John Bull as his chief Planner, Progress and Tool Design.

Having had some experience in each of these departments, as well as executive responsibility for all, at various later stages of my own career, it has long since been a matter of admiration how their relatively small staffs coped so successfully with the initial Spitfire production problems, whilst simultaneously handling the new Stranraer contract, the existing long running Walrus work and the new Walrus Development aircraft being built, not to mention the drawings already coming from the Design Office for Mitchell's four engined bomber, it is therefore fitting that Butler, Bull, Fred Amey, and Jack Knowles' contribution should be acknowledged, even at this late stage.

All the pre-production work eventually has to reach the manufacturing stages on the workshops floors and there the major responsibilities fall on the Foremen and the shop's Inspection.

When Pratt took over from Westbrook at the beginning of 1937 the Foremen were, Bill Heaver - hull or fuselages, Jim Weedy - wings and flying control surfaces on flying boats plus the Spitfire leading edge assembly, George Gingell - machine shop, Dick Earl - tool room, Frank Barnett - Electricians, Mr Camm - fittings and details, Bill Crooks - erecting shop, Harry Collins - Coppersmiths and tank shop, Harry Warren - woodshop and Len Levy in charge of the flight shed at Eastleigh. Miss Penton supervised the dope shop. These formed the hard-core, there were others who had various jobs which did not rate a foreman's white coat, but who nevertheless performed important functions in ways, like Sid Ings for painting aircraft, 'Ginger' Snelling in charge of the 'heavy gang' who provided the 'muscle power' when things had to be moved or lifted. Harry Gingell, brother to George, was in charge of the garage and transport. To the best of my knowledge all of these positions still held good up to the outbreak of war. No one who knew them will   disagree that they were a wildly disparate group, but each in his own way did a good job. In those days the foremen were responsible for the hiring and firing of their workers, seeing that no overloading of men occurred to increase the cost of any job, maintaining discipline, and ensuring that target dates were met. Closely working with them in respect of the latter requirement was the shop Progress Chaser - in the case of 'K' shop this was Jim Smith - and of course their charge hands - in 'K' shop again this was Bill Peckham. Below these were the 'leading hands': skilled men in various categories of their shops work content, but far too numerous to mention, who controlled small sections of workers and received two pence per hour extra to their basic pay for this service, which had to be performed whilst carrying out their own skilled work.

Chronologically we have now reached in to the early months of 1937 and I trust the reader has a reasonable idea of the circumstances that pertained in this respect of the overall scene and now we must return to the fuselage build in the first of the two jigs.

The rivetted structure was reinstalled, and checked again by the Inspector (Con Mann) and as in the intervening time the skin

The fuselage build line at Woolston Works. Vickers.

plating details had arrived this operation was commenced. Bill Heaver carefully selected the men he wanted for this task and if my memory serves me right the forward end plating was fitted by Bill Nicholas and Eddie Welsh. Who did the remainder is lost in the mists of time to me as at the time I was heavily engaged on the Stranraer flying boat hull on the opposite side of the workshop. Naturally, especially during our lunch breaks, the first production Spitfire fuselage was an object of continuing interest as we followed its progression through its plating and subsequent riveting (done by the Diaper brothers who were reckoned to be the best in the works, and justifiably so) then the fitting of the rear spar attachment fitting until at last, after much inspecting and ensuring that the main jig points were not 'binding' on their location pins and that nothing untoward happened when the jig control point pins and bolts were removed, the day arrived when it was removed from the building jig. Ginger Snelling and his gang with additional hands from our own men gently eased the shining silver fuselage out of the jig and on to the special trestles that had been made to hold it. There was no cheering or celebration; to us it was just another manhandling out of jig similar to the many Walruses and Scapas that had been manhandled before.

There was still quite a bit of work for my shop to do before the fuselage would be handed over to the Erecting shop for its internal installations etc. to commence.

Perhaps it will be easier for the reader to follow these jobs if I project our narrative forwards to the 24th fuselage where I began my personal involvement with the Spitfire on the 27th February 1938.

In the intervening period more fuselage jigs had been erected down the side of 'K' shop and the original assemblers were systematically divided as the work content increased so that the original pairs were split and each took under his wing a mid term apprentice or handy lad to teach them the operation on which they were engaged. Once learned these too were again split and the younger people were paired with others in the same age groups until something like eight different teams were allocated to each main fuselage assembly operation. I was switched from the Stranraer to join Arthur Newland as one of the rear, top bottom and side shell plating teams.

The build by then had settled as follows. Once the jig itself had been checked by a tool-maker after the previous fuselage had been removed, the retaining pins greased afresh and the profile plates oiled for ease of up and down movements, the Inspector would verify that it was to his satisfaction and inform the charge hand or leading hand that it was ready for use.

The first thing in the jig was always the front fireproof bulkhead Frame 5 which was located on the simulated wing spar fittings with their under size holes for later reaming out of jig, and the engine mounting simulated fittings. This frame was the heaviest of the fuselage sub-assemblies and required two men to instal into the jig. Simultaneously the rear attachment frame 19 would be bolted to its jig support, thus making the two ends of the fuselage's boundary. Frames 6 to 10 were next loaded and the forward bottom longerons and the datum longerons on each side were attached to the frame 5 bulkhead and to each individual frame. At a later stage frames 6 to 10 and the bottom longerons were made a sub-assembly which cut down this assembly in jig time. There was a joint in the bottom longeron at frame 10 which allowed a different section longeron to be fitted which then extended right back to affix to frame 19. The remaining frames were then loaded into the jigs, picking up pre-drilled holes at their locations on the top and bottom profile plates and the other longerons to which was now added the top longeron from frame 11 to frame 19. Frame 11 is the one immediately behind the pilot's seat.

This structure was then rivetted, and bearing in mind that these are inspection stages to be cleared between all of these operations, I shall not mention them again.

The front and rear fuselage plating teams would then move in to carry out their operations with just a short space between them so that the front 'skinners' could get the two bottom plates properly located enough so the rear 'skinners' could make the end of the front's panels their abutment point. The bottom front panels were in two halves, a buttstrap joining them along the fuselages centre line, and extending outwards to follow the frame contours until they were some six inches or so up each side. Once this was set in position they could continue with the other two side panels each side which stretched back to frame 12, thus when their work was done the bottom plates extended back to frame 11, and the sides to frame 12, and four of them fitting to frame 5 at the front. Because of the loads that they were to carry these front skins were thicker than any of the rear fuselage skins and were held by larger diameter rivets, in some cases snap head rivets which stood proud of the skins but were considerably stronger. By contrast, excepting for those attaching the skins to the main longerons, were all countersunk to decrease as much as possible any interference with a smooth air flow. Tests carried out on the prototype had shown that the rivet heads that protruded above skin surface level reduced the aircraft's speed by something like 5 mph, and everything was done to reduce this. Dome headed rivets were introduced, and wherever it was possible to countersink flush rivets were used. This was fairly easy where the skins were 18 SWG or more, but below that there was hardly enough skin thickness to use standard countersinking tools. Spin dimpling was introduced so that the thinner skins lost none of their strength from their thickness but could be countersunk without creating a weakness that could not be tolerated. These technical details, and many similar ones can be found in Morgan & Shacklady's 'Spitfire - The History' and Alfred Price's 'The Spitfire Story' and do not require repeating here.

I am on firmer ground in respect of the rear fuselage plating which no doubt the reader would like to know how it was tackled by two eighteen year olds. The top, bottom and side plating is easily identified from photographs or drawings of the Spitfire as it consisted of all shell skinning from frame 12 aft to the tail units transport joint at frame 19 with the exception of each upper front side panel which extended forwards to frame 11 so that it could incorporate the Hood sliding rails at a later stage. Fourteen panels all told, three along the bottom, four along each side, and a further three along the top. All the panels were pre-drilled in jigs after shaping and the sides and bottoms had their stringer stiffeners prefitted and rivetted. The longerons and frames were undrilled so the majority of panel positioning had to come from our pencilled lines down the centre of the frame and longeron flanges. The frames had the stringer attachment brackets prefitted so that we knew from these where the panel was located, but it did require us to sight through the pre-drilled skin holes our pencil centre lines on frames to ensure that we were not too far forwards or backwards which would result in either insufficient landing or a hole drilled too far into the frame's heel, with consequent scrap.

The prefitted stringers were invariably too long at each end which frustrated this aligning and we soon found that it was necessary to chip just a three-thirty-second of an inch sliver off the stringer flanges which was achieved by a sharp tap with a cold chisel whilst the panels outer face was held closely to a steel block with a polished surface so that no damage was incurred. We would start with the three bottom panels and once they were drilled and service bolted we switched to the three top panels and did likewise. Next we would do one side where the overlapping edges were undrilled at their top and bottom skin locations as the holes were already pre-drilled in the top and bottom skins. There were no butt joints in the skinning so that where an overlap occurred one panel would have the appropriate edge left blank to receive the hole position from the panel that overlapped it. Extra material would be left on the receiving skin so that a proper 'landing' could be marked off and cut in accordance with the drawing's requirement. Due to the narrow confines of the fuselage's from frame 11 aft it was beneficial to complete one side set of panels, including cutting the access doors with the aid of templates (on the port side the radio bay access above the datum longeron between frames 13 and 14, and on the starboard side the battery access door of similar size and shape just above the bottom longeron at frames 17 and 18) having this half skinning inspected, then remove so that accessibility to the opposite side was easier. When all the drilling had been completed, and the cutlines marked off in pencil the only drilling left was the stringer attachments to the frames. This was because the holes were only three-thirty-second in diameter, pre-drilled in the stringers themselves at the panel's sub assembly stage, and were more conveniently 'punched' in with a special small tool by the rivetters.

Just as the chaps on the front fuselage skinning operations, we on the rear end would then strip the whole of the plating off to clear away drilling swarf, remove any drilling burrs, and generally ensure that all the hole landings were correct, and definitely no double-holes were present. There would then be an inspection stage before re-assembly.

Before re-assembly all the mating surfaces would be given a coat of ghastly yellow coloured anti-corrosive paint. The sequence for re-assembly was much as before although at each of the two door apertures we had previously marked out and cut required that their door landing surrounds had to be fitted between frame and skin so that they were rivetted together at the same time. After these door frames were rivetted it was also part of our operation to fit the doors and their hinges, filing to suit where necessary and maintaining the gap required by the drawings to ensure free movement. The radio door was held open by a small strut as it opened upwards, but the battery door swung downwards and was supported by a couple of waxed string lanyards that we used to make by plaiting.

The complete riveting followed, generally by two squads, one for the forward end and the other for the rear. The final, in jig, act would be to position the fuselage datum plate on its starboard side as determined from the drawing dimensions and a piano wire stretched from jig points for the purpose from the front to rear of their structure.

Removal of the completed assembly was always done by manpower, and normally necessitated assistance from the shop labourers and some of the fuselage builders. Once safely removed the fuselage was placed on two supporting trestles, one under frame 5 picking up the machined metal pads that were a permanent fixture for the aircraft's maintenance, and the other a padded cradle shaped to suit the contours at frame 18 plus a strap that went around the fuselage at that end which was secured to a floor fixing.

Usually there would be a short 'dressing' operation to remove any slight deviations that might have occurred during riveting, but once this was done operations were commenced to fit the cockpit door and the hood rails so that they aligned (the top of the door was part of the rail) and with these locations established follow straight through with the fittings of the cockpit coaming, the windscreen, and the sliding hood. There were also a lot of what I term 'bitty' jobs that could only be done out of jig such as cutting the hole for the aerial mast and fitting the nut-plates for its support, fitting stiffeners to parts where early modifications called for them, e.g. between frames 12 and 13, and for the tail parachute location as well as the upwards identification lamp mounting. Most of these jobs we young lads would do whilst waiting for another fuselage to skin, often they only took less than a quarter of an hour and our charge hand would give us job cards to do batches of anything from five to ten off, dependent on how long he thought it would be before we could return to our main task.

One very important operation needed to be carried out before the fuselage could be moved from 'K' shop and on to the erection shop where as much of its internal fittings such as, electrics, hydraulics, fuel tanks, pneumatics, etc. would be added, and that was to place the now near completed fuselage shell into a special jig created for the interchange repeatability requirements between fuselage and wing.

This jig incorporated not only the positioning of the nut-plate attachments for the eventual wing-to-fuselage fairing fillet panels, but more importantly allowed the opening up of the undersized holes at the wing spar attachments at frame five which had hitherto been used as jig locations in the main build jig to their fully reamed size. These holes were critical to the wing fit and necessitated them to be an 'A', or 'push' fit so that when the wings were offered to the fuselage the locating pins (again subject to a close tolerance size) could be driven home through the wings leading edge holes (equally a fine fit required) and secured by nuts at the rear ends. These nuts were screwed on to the threaded portion of the pins which had been specifically designed and made so that the thread was smaller than the pins diameter and allowed a soft metal 'bullet' to be screwed over them which protected the reamed holes as they were driven home. Once in position these bullets would be removed and the securing nuts fitted and torque loaded followed by the drilling and fixing of the castle headed nuts with split pinning.

By and large the method of fuselage building described remained the same, with minor adjustments, throughout the whole production of the Spitfire, wherever it was built.

The wing however proved to be a different problem. There was, as

Part of the Spitfire Wing Shop at Woolston. Vickers.

I have mentioned, some delay due to the modifications required by the Ministry and although once these had been incorporated on the drawings and acted on, particularly in respect of the supplier of the present leading edge skins, the Woolston shop under Jim Weedy proceeded with the torsion box manufacture, but only for supply to the wing subcontractors that had been insisted upon by the Air Ministry because of the Supermarine's lack of production capacity. The subcontractors too were not without their problems, dealing as they were with an aircraft and type of construction with which they were largely unfamiliar. These problems were compounded by, what with the blessing of hindsight, appears to have been poor liaison, and made worse from what I can gather from information given to me, the loss of many query notes that occurred when the design department moved to their brand new design office block. I am not aware of what arrangements were made in respect of design liaison, but I feel sure that the wing subcontractors must have been disadvantaged by the unfamiliar query note procedure and no doubt delays that might easily have arisen if these queries were answered through the normal postal system.

In the past fifty years sufficient evidence has come to light which explains some of the frustrations and delays which severely affected the Supermarine operations and hampered production pre-war.

In the first instance it now appears that the Air Ministry itself was not totally sold on the production of the Spitfire and after placing its initial order was very reluctant to follow it up, thus causing the Vickers aircraft managing director, Sir Robert McLean, to (a) delay the removal of the flying boat work that was still occupying precious factory floor space and (b) not to be sure that the whole production facility would not be utilised for producing either Beaufighters or Whirlwinds.

However, in the interim, until these matters were resolved, the Wing shop personnel continued with their leading edges; making the detail parts on the balcony over 'K' shop where the rib drawn sections were contoured in Ted Gardener's section and then be subassembled by the girls further along the balcony working under the supervision of Ted Taylor and Bill Mills. (A drawn section was an angle, or lipped angle, or even channel section as formed by the 'Drawbenches' at the river end of 'K' shop, but operated as a section of the wing shop under Chris Parker, where coiled strip rolls of suitably sized alclad were clamped into the machines jaws and pulled mechanically through a series of rollers to form the desired section in lengths of approximately twenty-five feet.)

It was due to these subcontracting hiccups and our own only partial wing assembly - the torsion box - that the fuselage shells began to accumulate in the Woolston Erection shop at the end of 1937 and early 1938 with the inevitable critical comments made by the Air Ministry representatives who appeared from time to time to see the progress of their order. The outcome was an instruction to off-load the flying boat work - with the exception of the Walrus Development, later better known as the Sea Otter - and erect our own wing building jigs. This all took valuable time, and some idea of the controversy that raged around these decisions can be read in some detail in Alfred

The Design office etc. looking down Hazel Road towards the Floating Bridge end. Vickers.

The Main Stores entrance Woolston from Hazel Road. Vickers.

Price's excellent book, 'The Spitfire Story'. In those accounts one can sense the urgency of the hour and the frustration at delays as the International situation was moving inexorably towards war.

By the time that most of the building works on factory extensions had been finished - and this was not until late 1938 - the format of the Spitfire production line had been settled in the manner it was to proceed throughout its manufacturing life.

Fuselages were shipped to the Itchen works where the subcontracted rear fuselage empennages were joined to them, whatever system could be safely installed were added, and the engine cradle support mountings fitted.

Wings, once they became available from the subcontractors, prior to our own build that followed, went directly to Eastleigh as did the engines, propellers, wing tips etc. There the final assembly of the components took place, the testing of the various systems,

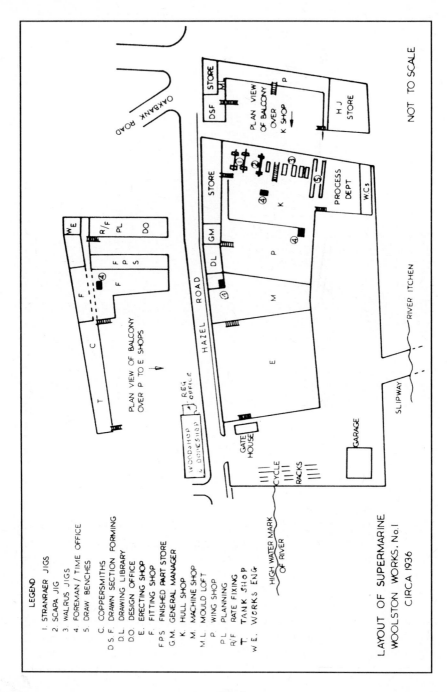

LEGEND

1. STRANRAER JIGS
2. SCAPA JIG
3. WALRUS JIGS
4. FOREMAN / TIME OFFICE
5. DRAW BENCHES

C. COPPERSMITHS
D.S.F. DRAWN SECTION FORMING
D.L. DRAWING LIBRARY
D.O. DESIGN OFFICE
E. ERECTING SHOP
F. FITTING SHOP
FPS FINISHED PART STORE
G.M. GENERAL MANAGER
K. HULL SHOP
M. MACHINE SHOP
M.L. MOULD LOFT
P. WING SHOP
PL. PLANNING
R/F RATE FIXING
T. TANK SHOP
W.E. WORKS ENG

LAYOUT OF SUPERMARINE
WOOLSTON WORKS. No.1
CIRCA 1936

NOT TO SCALE

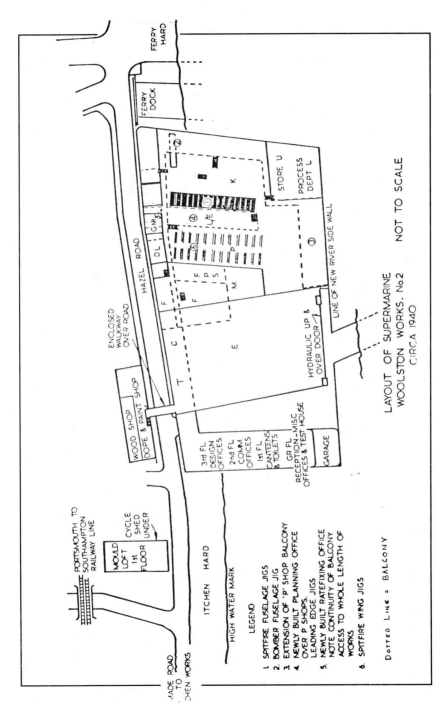

LAYOUT OF SUPERMARINE
WOOLSTON WORKS. No 2   NOT TO SCALE
CIRCA 1940

LEGEND

1. SPITFIRE FUSELAGE JIGS
2. BOMBER FUSELAGE JIG
3. EXTENSION OF 'P' SHOP BALCONY
4. NEWLY BUILT PLANNING OFFICE
   OVER P SHOPS.
   LEADING EDGE JIGS
5. NEWLY BUILT RATEFIXING OFFICE
   NOTE CONTINUITY OF BALCONY
   ACCESS TO WHOLE LENGTH OF
   WORKS
6. SPITFIRE WING JIGS

DOTTED LINE = BALCONY

then the push out of the hangar for the ground running of the Rolls-Royce engine to the satisfaction of the Roll's representative, a final inspection clearance by Works and Air Ministry Inspectors, prior to its hand over to the test pilot for its maiden flight. When necessary the test pilot would ask for adjustments to be made, mostly minor ones, and in my experience generally to the trailing edge of the ailerons if the aircraft showed a tendency to fly one wing down. Once cleared, the A.I.D. would sign the necessary paperwork so that the aircraft could be delivered to wherever the R.A.F. required it.

That, very broadly, was the situation prevailing up to the outbreak of war, and continued until enemy action enforced a certain number of relocations.

My personal contact with the Spitfire fuselage plating operations, explained earlier, ceased in January 1939 when I transferred to other work, as detailed in Spitfire Odyssey, but before leaving that subject there is one other item that needs to be clarified. The High Speed Spitfire.

There is extant the story that a fuselage was taken out of the normal production line and modified afterwards to suit the High Speed design. This is not so. Two fuselages, numbers 48 and 49, were pre-allocated for the purpose and during their normal build cycle steel channel stiffeners were fitted to the insides of the datum longerons, and some of the skin plating panels we fitted were of a thicker gauge material than the norm. Oswald Scott and his partner named Barker did number 48 which was the one finally selected to become the High Speed Spitfire, whilst Arthur Newland and myself did number 49 which eventually continued on the production line and became a service aircraft, albeit far stronger than I expect the pilot ever guessed. The numbers I have quoted are the shop building sequence numbers only. In 'Spitfire - The History' the High Speed aircraft is given as number 35, but this number only arises because of the High Speed aircraft being advanced at Eastleigh for its special purpose.

All told I had spent nearly a year on the plating job and it may be of interest to readers to know something about the young men who carried out the rear plating operations I have described.

Firstly, we were mostly in the eighteen to twenty years age group and our pay was at eighteen, sixpence (2½p) per hour, rising in the next year to seven pence three farthings per hour, then annually, dependent on the relevant birthday, up to nine pence halfpenny, to ten pence farthing (roughly 4p in present currency). Those were the apprentice rates, the skilled men were on one shilling and four pence halfpenny when I joined the Company in 1936, but successive nationally agreed increments increased this figure to one shilling and ten pence per hour when I achieved my own skilled status in 1941.

Those were the 'basic' rates but all operations in the workshops were subject to a bonus scheme which was based on rate fixed times. Details of how this scheme was operated are contained in 'Spitfire Odyssey' and therefore not repeated here, other than to add that from my first introduction to rear fuselage plating until I left it eleven months later, Arthur Newland and I had completed 63 fuselages, the first having taken us 115 hours and at the end we were comfortably doing the same task in well under half that time and thus earning 'time and a half' which enhanced our pay by roughly another penny per hour less than the basic rate.

Similar results applied throughout the works with bonus pay directly related to production effort to skilled and semi-skilled men and also to the women and girls at their particular tasks. A few squabbles were inevitable with the person who fixed the rates - the rate fixer - but by and large these were soon settled and although initially many thought they had been hard done by when 'push came to shove' mostly people found that some bonus could be earned and in the circumstances prevailing at the time with over two million unemployed seeking work felt that a bird in the hand was worth two in the proverbial bush.

This became most evident after the Munich Agreement, when despite all the professed 'peace in our time' propaganda it slowly but remorsefully dawned on all but the most unsusceptible that it was just the prelude to war, and with the greater urgency placed on production, the allocation of further contracts once the Air Council had made its mind up that Spitfires were required, the increased efforts by the works to produce them was reflected in still higher levels of bonus earnings.

By that fateful Sunday when war was declared just over three hundred of the original 310 order had been completed and taken on charge by the R.A.F./Air Ministry and the second order for a further 200 was well advanced.

Thus the scene was set that was to affect almost every member of Supermarines, as indeed it did for so many others all across the world.

With the inevitability of the coming war becoming apparent further orders for Spitfires materialised and although we were still restricted very largely by floor space every other effort known to the production planning team was employed.

Sub-assemble! became the magic word to overcome some of the problems associated by the inability to lay down any more main assembly jigs.

Overtime hours and night shifts were enhanced. In the year 1938 the working week was 50 hours, but in 1939 both day and night shifts were upgraded to 63 hours per week and by June 1940, when Dunkirk became a name to be remembered the working week was raised to seven days and 70 hours on day shift and 73 on nights.

On the sub-assembly side it was found that, on the fuselage for instance, the frames and connecting longerons between frames 11 and 19 could be rivetted together prior to their insertion into the main jig by their pre-drilling. Similarly the frames 6 to 10 could be sub-assembled with their different longeron assemblies and at a later date it was found possible to prefit to this latter sub-assembly the two main bottom skins and their connecting buttstrap joints.

Similar procedures took place wherever possible on the wings. Instead of as originally building the leading edges from spar booms up and adding the ribs and skins with their subsequent riveting in the one jig it was possible to make spar booms complete with their web plates separately, followed by another differently located operation to add the ribs, and finally use a main jig to fix and rivet the skins.

Using these methods, and many such others, plus the increased working hours, the production figures soon rose quite substantially.

According to the information made known to me on the first order for 310 Spitfires the Company averaged just over five per week, whereas in the quarter before we were bombed 360 Spitfires were produced, an average of 30 per week.

Once the declaration of war was announced any previous production programmes that had applied were forgotten. The need was there to get as many Spitfires and Hurricanes available for the battles that must lay in the future.

Supermarines lacked the resources available to Hawker's who had much more production capacity to hand, even to setting up a production line in Canada where they had interests.

Supermarines could not expect any help from Weybridge as they were fully occupied with their bomber programme.

It has been said "that the first casualty of war is truth" and an example of the type of propaganda nonsense we were to be subjected to is still being shown on television occasionally today in respect of the Vickers Wellington bomber. Entitled, something like, 'Built in twenty four hours' it pretends to portray that a Wellington was assembled from sub-assemblies, its fabric coverings over its Geodetic structure fitted and doped, engines and all internal fittings fixed and tested, systems tested prior to first flight, and then lo' and behold we are shown the aircraft taking off twenty-four hours later to the cheers of the assembled workers.

What a load of nonsense! Anyone in the aircraft industry will tell you that it would take all of that time and more just to apply the fabric covering to the structure and allow it to dry. This is in no way implying anything detrimental to the efforts of Vickers production team, but does serve to illustrate the type of rubbish being fed to the public in general by the Ministry of Information to 'boost our morale?'

Unfortunately similar misinformation and downright deception was

SPITFIRE MAIN FUSELAGE

FRAMEWORK

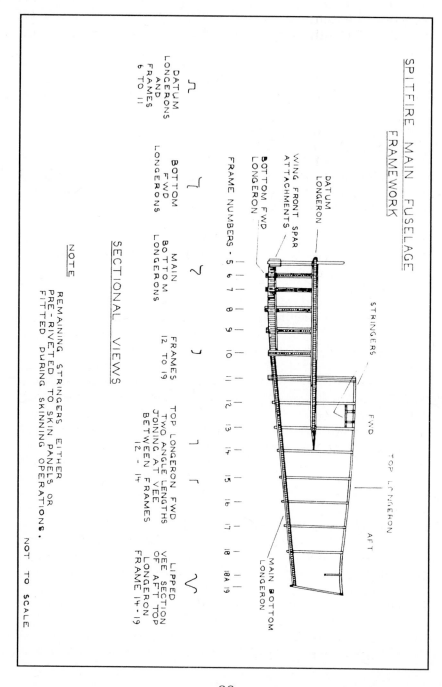

DATUM
LONGERONS
AND
FRAMES
6 TO 11

DATUM
LONGERONS

WING FRONT SPAR
ATTACHMENTS

BOTTOM FWD
LONGERON

FRAME NUMBERS - 5 6 7 8 9 10 11 12 13 14 15 16 17 18 18A 19

DATUM
LONGERON

STRINGERS

FWD

TOP LONGERON

AFT

MAIN BOTTOM
LONGERON

BOTTOM
FWD
LONGERONS

MAIN
BOTTOM
LONGERONS

FRAMES
12 TO 19

TOP LONGERON FWD
TWO ANGLE LENGTHS
JOINING AT VEE
BETWEEN FRAMES
12 - 14

LIPPED
VEE SECTION
OF AFT TOP
LONGERON
FRAME 14 - 19

SECTIONAL VIEWS

NOTE

REMAINING STRINGERS EITHER
PRE-RIVETED TO SKIN PANELS OR
FITTED DURING SKINNING OPERATIONS.

NOT TO SCALE

applied to the Spitfire production; some of which is still toted around as the truth today. Wherever I can, I hope to dispel some of these myths.

More fortunately, once war was declared the natural pragmatic instincts of Supermarines top management came to the fore. As previously indicated space was at a premium and Mr. Pratt in conjunction with Wilfred Elliot set their sights in obtaining more of this valuable commodity. Early in December 1939 a bay at one end of the disused Rolling Mills on the Weston shore was taken over (the Admiralty grabbed the rest for its storage purposes) and despite its condition - especially the roof - as soon as it was made serviceable most of the coppersmiths and tank shop under Harry Collins were transferred there.

The Electric Joinery Works at Newtown was taken over completely as our Woodshop under the supervision of Harry Warren at almost the same time .

I am reliably informed by someone who was present at the time that in the early thirties the Air Ministry suggested that both Vickers Weybridge and Supermarines at Southampton should move to 'safer' areas. A map, purporting to show the desirable areas was supplied and the firms asked to submit their recommendations. Trevor Westbrook went site searching and eventually thought that a site near Flint on the river Dee Estuary might be suitable where both airfield and flying boat facilities were possible. However, as no-one appeared to offer the financing of such moves the whole matter was eventually shelved. I suppose that had Westbrook succeeded in his plans there would have been no Woolston, Itchen or Weybridge works to bomb, but I'm sure in the end it would have been to little avail once the Germans had overrun France and the whole of the coasts to the north.

Once the battle of France was over and the retreat from Dunkirk the best salvage operation our forces could do it was plain to all that the next target for the Germans was to defeat this country - and bombing was obviously going to be their opening gambit.

There is a saying that truth is stranger than fiction but at the time the coppersmiths moved into the Weston Shore Rollings Mills no-

one would have guessed that five years later they would be obliged
by the Ministry for Aircraft Production to evacuate the building on
security grounds so that the build-up of the Invasion fleet of tank
landing and other craft could proceed. They were temporarily located for about three months in various units in other areas.

Chapter two - Production and Air Raids

At the time of the Munich Agreement only 7 Spitfires had been delivered to the R.A.F., according to the chart compiled from the Supermarine company records, with a further 4 delivered to Boscombe Down, Martlesham Heath, or retained at Eastleigh for Manufacturers Trials. The fact that over 300 had been delivered by the outbreak of hostilities is the measure for the breathing space Neville Chamberlain's sad appeasement policy gave us. A year later, again using the same chart, with the Battle of Britain nearly over, and by the time that production ceased at Woolston and Itchen, this production total had reached 1,198 delivered.

It took a little while to clear the production snags, but once the subcontractors were contributing their share, and the wing build line had been established at Woolston, the flow of aircraft through the Eastleigh hangar increased immensely.

For those who are interested in the Supermarine production figures the following page is a copy of the graph that was compiled from the register of deliveries made and held in the General Manager's office at Woolston and subsequently at Hursley Park. So far as I am aware this is the first time this chart has ever been published, and I am indebted to a senior member of the Company for it. The fact that it survives is by pure chance as the register was itself almost lost at the time of the move to South Marston after the war, but was rescued (?) by my benefactor.

Behind the early production figures mentioned above lies the story of another 'battle' fought much earlier by Sir Robert McLean of Vickers which deserves its place in this postscript.

Getting orders for new aircraft, as I know from experience elsewhere, is sometimes a difficult, time consuming, and delicate job, fraught with all manner of pitfalls, especially when it comes down to price and delivery dates. Quite often promises have to be made to obtain a contract that are known to be very unlikely to be fulfilled - not with any evil intent to mislead - but because, by the very nature of aircraft production being always at the forefront of the latest technology no one really knows what may occur to upset the best estimates made at the time.

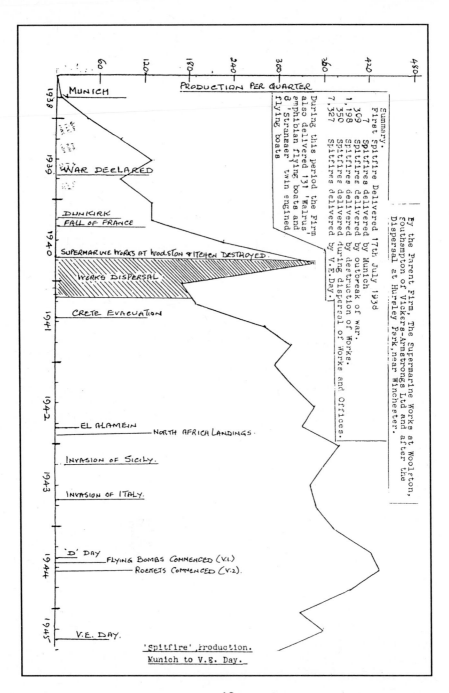

'Spitfire' Production. Munich to V.E. Day.

Sir Robert, as Chairman of Vickers Aviation Division was a man at the time that the Spitfire was born, whose track record had to be acknowledged. Apparently, as early as 1931, he was convinced that a European War was certain to come, and in spite of the recession of those days he began to rebuild and modernise the Supermarine Works that they had purchased the controlling interest in 1928. At Weybridge they had tendered for a Light Bomber and got the contract, but Sir Robert, with his Design team which included Barnes -Wallis, thought the Ministry Specification, which was for a biplane was out of date and proceeded to design and build at the Company's expense what eventually became the 'Wellesley' - the first of the geodetic type structure that led on to the Wellington. The test flights for this monoplane proved highly successful and Sir Robert tried to get the contract changed, but the Air Ministry would not listen - shades of what was to happen again later with the Spitfire!

Sir Robert then wrote direct to Air Marshal Sir Hugh Dowding, then the Director of Research and Development, and the important part reads:-
'I suggest to you that it might be better to reduce those orders in numbers (for the biplane) and in their place go into production on the monoplane as soon as tooling can be completed. Meanwhile, and until you decide whether we shall be allowed to switch over from the biplane to the monoplane, I do not wish to proceed with the work on the biplane because in my view it is not a modern machine'.
It takes a lot of courage to write in that manner to your best customer, but it worked, and on September 10th 1935 Vickers got the order to drop the biplane and build 79 'Wellesleys'.

At Supermarines Sir Robert sanctioned the building of the 'Walrus' type amphibian despite the Air Ministry stating in writing 'that they saw no use for such an aircraft.' Fortunately the Naval Admirals did like it, and forced a purchase for trials which resulted in the Australians buying it as the 'Seagull' and in the end some 700 all told were built.

Something similar happened in respect of the 'Stranraer' flying boat when the first one was built as a 'private venture' and eventually Supermarine received an order for 17, and Canadian Vickers built another 40.

The initial design for the prototype Spitfire was funded as a 'private venture', although the Air Ministry very soon covered it with a contract.

Sadly, as so often occurs when one is invariably right in dealing with high officials in Ministries, when Sir Charles Craven took over as Controller of Aircraft Production in the Beaverbrook Ministry of Aircraft Production (Sir Charles had been Chairman of Vickers Shipbuilding and Engineering prior to that) he thought Sir Robert ran the risk of upsetting the 'Top Brass' and they parted company.

However, before that Sir Robert had stated to the Air Ministry that 'Provided that the Contractors' trials (on the prototype Spitfire) were completed by the end of March 1936, Martlesham trials by April 1936, and a production order placed by May 1st 1936, the firm should be able to start production of the single seat fighter in 15 months, i.e. September 1937, at the rate of 5 per week. In this event it should be possible to turn out a total of between 360 and 380 by 31st March 1939.'

When one considers that the order was not placed until June 1936, and more importantly, the Specification not delivered to the Company until July 1936, the fact that 306 were delivered by 3rd September 1939 cannot be considered 'wildly inaccurate' has been stated elsewhere.

Without Sir Robert McLean's backing the genius of R. J. Mitchell might never have been released to create the masterpiece with which his name will forever be associated. On this score alone Sir Robert deserves to be remembered as one who this country owes a lot.

The gathering pace of Spitfire production is clear from the records of Supermarine which show that the original requirement for 5 per week was soon exceeded once the initial snags had been overcome. The monthly output for 1940 was as follows:- Jan 37, Feb 45, Mar 42, Apr 60, May 77, Jun 94, July 134, Aug 128, Sept 103, Oct 53, Nov 73, Dec 42. The fall-off after September reflects the effect of the bombing of the Woolston and Itchen Works on September 26th 1940, and the delays incurred whilst a dispersal plan was put into operation.

The chart shows dramatically the time it took to re-establish the full production again. Bearing in mind that for some reason it is marked off in quarter year periods it nevertheless shows that the upward trend did not commence until the end of 1940 and the earlier peak was not reached until roughly the middle of 1942. This might have had a very serious effect on the containment of the war had not the 'shadow factory' at Castle Bromwich at last begun to produce Spitfires and justify the vast investment that had been created for it, but more of that later.

Once the Germans had reorganised themselves after the fall of France and the Low Countries their bombers were free to launch their attacks on the British Isles as a prelude to their intended invasion plans. The story of that period and its subsequent history has been told far more eloquently and in much greater detail and authority elsewhere. One thing was immediately obvious to all was that no part of the United Kingdom was beyond the reach of their bombers and that as a legitimate target we at Supermarines must be on the list.

Preparations had been made, buildings were camouflaged, shelters built, ARP services organised and anti-aircraft gun sites established, but as someone prewar had said in Parliament, "the bomber will always get through" and so far the history of war has proved that. One of the disadvantages of being where we were was that the configuration of the location with its land shapes and waterside proximity made the site fairly easily identifiable from aircraft.

How and why they left us alone for so long has always been a source of amazement to me. I can only conclude, like so many others have, that either their High Command, under the direction of Goering, was unsoundly based, or that there was something seriously wrong with their intelligence system. Had they put us out of action in June 1940 by destroying the Eastleigh hangars and the works at Woolston and Itchen then the whole course of the Battle of Britain might have been different and a successful invasion achieved. This is in no way intended to belittle the Hawker Hurricane and its magnificent achievements, especially during the Battle of Britain, but it is now commonly accepted that the Spitfire's performance was more equal to the ME 109, the then current fighter for the Luftwaffe, which had a degree of superiority over the Hurricane which may have proved just too much without the support service rendered by the Spitfire.

Southampton's first visitation by enemy bombers came on the night of the 19th June 1940 when a lone aircraft dropped a stick of bombs that straddled the lower end of Regents Park Road and out towards Marchwood. Damage was caused to residential properties, a filling station in Millbrook Road and generally alerted the town that the war was virtually on their doorstep now. That particular air raid alarm lasted for 6 hours from 11-10 pm, which meant that generally people would be in their shelters, but worse that night production of all kinds in factories and elsewhere would have ceased. This loss of production time through one aircraft in this instance was to become an important factor later and the introduction of new procedures.

From that moment on there were alarms on an almost daily basis, some when it transpired the Southampton area was not involved, but this was a new phenomenon and those responsible for Air Raid Precautions had to feel their way in dealing with it. During this period we had emergency evacuation exercises to test the shelter facilities that had been made. These shelters were located on the lower edge of Peartree Green in front of the Itchen Works but accessed through a narrow brick archway that supported the railway lines running on the embankment that it carried. The first practice evacuation of the works showed this to be a potential hazard by slowing the numbers wishing to reach the shelters. It also took the Woolston employees anything up to five minutes to reach their designated shelter. These two factors, and the relatively close proximity of the shelters to the Itchen site - an obvious target - persuaded a good number of us to reject the idea of using the Company shelters. It proved very fortunate that we did. Time loss was to be reduced by an internal warning system and on August 13th the works klaxons sounded to tell the employees to evacuate the works. This day I made my way up Ferry Hill and on to the Peartree Green just alongside the Church from which vantage point a good view over Southampton was obtained. There was a very low cloud base, probably no more than a thousand feet, and consequently when the German squadrons of bombers and fighters passed overhead - en route for their intended target of the Middle Wallop airfield - it was impossible for ground observers to see them, but the noise, and the estimation that could be made from it of the numbers, filled me with apprehension.

Fortunately the enemy force was intercepted north of Southampton and from the ground could clearly be heard the sounds of battle. The sounds that had hardly passed over my location were now returning and by the screaming and firing noises in some confusion. My concern then was that the fleeing bombers might just ditch their loads because some of the conflict was obviously right overhead. There was no place to run, nothing to do but just sweat it out and hope for the best.

Suddenly two bombers, JU88's I believe, shot out from the base of the clouds over the town and let go their loads. By pure luck the International Cold Store in Southampton docks took a direct hit from one plane which took fire and with its stock of meats and fats blazed away for a week. Having witnessed this episode you can imagine my surprise when long after the war I saw a copy of the German Luftwaffe's magazine 'Der Adler' with a reconnaissance photograph showing the burnt out Cold Store with the following caption in English (for the benefit of the USA market at the time) "This photograph brought back by a reconnaissance plane proves convincingly the accuracy with which the German Air Force is able to hit vitally important plants". Some accuracy, and some propaganda!

After this the pace hotted up in our area, although ironically that same night the Castle Bromwich factory was bombed and ten workers killed with some damage to 'F' block which could not have helped either morale or production. Each day the air raid alarms were causing the loss of many hours of productive time. My diary says of one day, 'Five raids today - only did five hours work.' This could not be allowed to continue and the delayed warning system introduced was operated from within the works by observers on the roof in telephone communication with the area ARP control. August 14th brought another small raid which I believe to be intended for Eastleigh Airport but it was frustrated by anti-aircraft fire and the speedy raising of the balloon barrage which caused the bombers to drop their loads in the Bitterne Park/St. Denys area. One bomb actually landed on the railway track just outside St. Denys station as a train was approaching causing the driver to brake violently and come to a halt before reaching the damaged line.

The following day a sneak attack by a formation of ME 109's shot down seven barrage balloons as if clearing a corridor to the Woolston factory. On that same day ME 110's bombed within the London area and created the incident that led to our forces bombing Berlin and the diversion of the Luftwaffe's main activities in the reduction of the R.A.F.'s ability to defend by destroying airfields and aircraft factories, to Hitler's preferred propaganda response with the daylight bombing of London with the main weight of the German forces. The story of that prolonged and agonising period wherein the Battle of Britain was virtually decided and led into the imposition of the 'Blitz' at night has been adequately covered by many authors elsewhere.

For us at Southampton, and particularly for the production of Spitfires, the extra time this diversion gave us was a blessing. However, we did not get off scot free as a highly trained and daring German group, Erprobungsgruppe 210, had been specifically tasked to bomb the aircraft factories. Originally conceived as a replacement for the JU87 Stuka which was getting heavy losses when facing the Hurricanes and Spitfires, it began its early days with attacks on Channel shipping with some success using bomb armed ME 109's and ME 110's, then as the battle warmed up it was switched mainly to attack factories and radar sites.

In my book, 'Spitfire Odyssey', I have given accounts of my personal involvement in the raids that followed and I do not wish to repeat them here except where, in the interests of this broader canvas additional details are relevant.

Apart from a couple of abortive attempts by either single or pairs of bombers in making what might well have been intended attacks on either Eastleigh or Woolston aircraft centres the first real signs of aggression came on the 11th September when the ME 109's of

Erpro 210 screamed in low on Eastleigh Aerodrome and bombed the Cunliffe-Owen factory in mistake for the Spitfire final assembly and flight unit barely a stone's throw away. In that raid the death toll was about 50 due to a shelter being hit and others being unable to reach safety as they were caught above ground. I have placed the death toll at 'about 50' quite deliberately as even today, no one seems to be exactly sure in their reports and this method of approximation will apply to any further numbers in this fatality category.

Apparently the Cunliffe-Owen raid was carried out by the ME 109 squadron of Erpro 210 which comprised of nine aircraft, although accounts differ as to the actual number engaged in this attack. My personal information is that it was eight, one aircraft having been unserviceable. The Germans must have considered they had hit their intended target because, as mentioned earlier, no further attacks were made on the Spitfire hangars at Eastleigh.

It was not difficult to deduce that it was only a matter of time before they had a go at the Woolston and Itchen works and four days later, on September 15th, the first attack came. This time it was by at least 15 of the twin engined ME 110 which were able to carry two bombs as opposed to the 109's one. They bombed short and their target, the Woolston works was untouched, but grievous damage and casualties were incurred in Woolston itself, where one area was subsequently evacuated and used as a training ground for troops in house to house fighting. The official statistics quote 6 killed, 19 seriously injured and 23 injured, but I only saw two of the fatalities. The official damage figures for business and residential properties were 34 totally destroyed, 81 so badly damaged as to require demolition, 351 seriously damaged but capable of repair and 755 slightly damaged.

The weather deteriorated over the next few days and apart from the odd alarm caused by reconnaissance flights very little of consequence happened until the 24th, when two squadrons of the twin engined Me 110's of Erpro 210 once again directed their attack at the Woolston plants.

This time the internal raid warning for the works came too late and the employees took it upon themselves to depart in haste at the sound of gunfire, the louder blasts from the Netley Grange battery giving us just enough time to get outside, but only just. The Woolston people scattered in various places adjacent to the works (I only managed to make it as far as the gutter by the newsagents at the bottom of Oakbank Road, barely 20 yards from the works stores entrance through which I had fled) and some did not even get out at all, but fortunately for us the bombs were aimed at the Itchen works further up the road. Some thirty odd bombs fell, all missing their target but unfortunately managing to catch the Itchen staff as they made for the shelters when most of them were cramming the narrow archway that went under the railway line. Two bombs fell right into the archway entrance on the Works side and another had struck a shelter that was built into the Works perimeter fence. Two more over the railway bank side had struck the shelters and the remainder were scattered around, either on waste ground in Whites Shipyard, or on the wasteland below Peartree Green where the soggy nature of the soil absorbed their effect.

The Works rescue team from Woolston were quickly on the spot, joined by some of us who felt we might assist. The scene was chaotic as those who had had lucky escapes made haste to depart down

Photo taken from the top of the railway embankment opposite the Itchen Works showing some of the shelters damaged. Author.

the same narrow dirt roadway as the would-be rescuers tried to get to the scene of the disaster. The entrance to the archway was awful to contemplate. No one who has not witnessed the effects of high explosive on the human body can imagine what it was like. In films one sees people shot or blown up but they never show the horror of the terribly mutilated bodies as they lay scattered in their unidentifiable portions. The explosions had thrown some poor souls up on the railway embankment with the dirt from their craters and it was possible to see a limb poking out and hoping to rescue whoever might be covered by the dirt to discover it was just an unattached limb.

It soon became very obvious that the rescuers attentions would be better employed in releasing those trapped in the perimeter fence shelter which had been hit at its entrance end. In this we were more fortunate and although a few had been killed and a few injured, at least some had survived and these, with others who had not succumbed to the other bombs, we began to load on to the canvas covered ambulances that by now had arrived.

The raid had taken place at 1.30 pm and during the rescue work a German reconnaissance plane flew across to the east of us no doubt hoping to record the demise of the Spitfire factory.

The official ARP incident report gives the figures of 42 dead, 63 seriously injured and 98 with minor injuries. What the casualty list would have been had there been five minutes warning I hate to think because by then the bulk of the Woolston works would have been in that fateful spot.

What must have been galling to the Luftwaffe was the fact soon displayed by their reconnaissance photographs that the Spitfire factories at both Woolston and Itchen were still intact.

The next day almost all those who had escaped returned to work. A few, and not very many, stayed away because of shock and because they realised, as most of us did, that there must be more to come.

And come it did on the Thursday 26th September 1940.

This time we had plenty of warning which allowed those who chose to go to the shelters to do so, and others (like myself) to put a mile or so distance between ourselves and the works.

The raid came this time in two distinct waves and the bombing aircraft were mainly Heinkel 111's covered by escorting fighters. According to the best estimates available it is said that 200 bombs were dropped, 70 tons in all, but only seven struck the Woolston

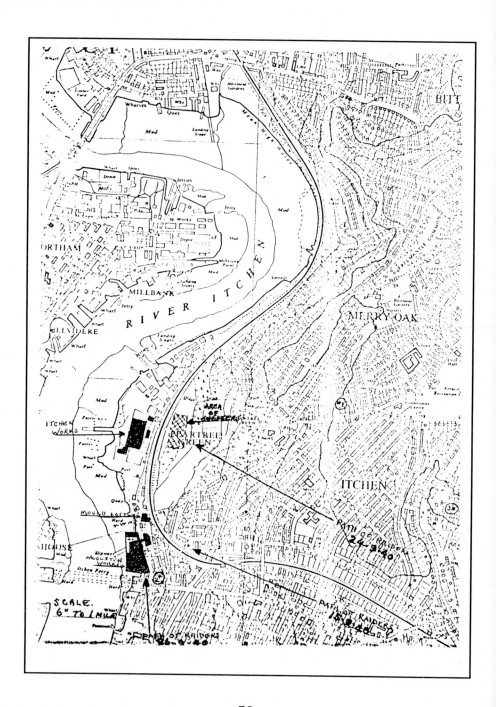

'P' shop balcony at the southern end of the Woolston Works after the 26th Sept. raid. Note that whilst the metal roof trusses are damaged the bomb appears to have dissipated its force into the air as the benches etc. below show little damage. Vickers.

THE ITCHEN ASSEMBLY UNIT
AFTER 26-9-40

The Itchen Works after the raid of the 26th. The shelter in the foreground
received a direct hit just out of picture. Vickers

works and just one the Itchen works. The damage considering the
strength of the bombing force was surprisingly slight. At Itchen
their one bomb had wrapped the fuselage of Mitchell's bomber
around a roof support stanchion and had written off about 23
Spitfire fuselages in various stages of out of jig assembly. All the

glasswork was broken and most of the roof covering with some of the lighter wall cladding had been demolished. Apart from the distorted roof truss where the bomb had entered the main walls and metal structure was intact. The shelter area was hit again and suffered some casualties.

At Woolston, the result looking at it from the German point of view would have been most discouraging. Again the glasswork and roofing had gone, but apart from one machine upended in the machine shop and the various relatively small damage caused by flying shrapnel, there did not seem to be an awful lot to worry about as mostly the major jigs and tooling had escaped almost scot free. The main walls were intact all round; the only real damage to brickwork had been by one of the bombs striking the waterside corner of the separate Design Office block.

I went into the factory on the following Saturday to collect my tools and was amazed that so big a raid in broad daylight with only anti-aircraft gunfire to impede them whilst their fighters kept our fighters away that so little real destruction had occurred. I was reminded of this only recently when watching a television documentary on our bombing of the Essen Krupps works. From our reconnaissance photos it shows one plant very much like ours must have looked - knocked out - but the worker who had been there and survived said "All they did was clear away the rubble and were back at work in three days."

Maybe we could have done something similar, after all it was still summertime so roof and windows were not terribly important. However Lord Beaverbrook came down to see the situation for himself that same Thursday evening and decided to go for a complete dispersal.

The casualties for this raid are given as 36 killed (approximately) and 60 seriously injured. The approximately tells its own story!

In view of what was to come it is now clear that Beaverbrook's decision was the right one as once the serious night bombing commenced the risks would have been unacceptable.

Once again we can refer via 'Der Adler' for enlightenment from the

Bomb damage in the Woolston Works machine shop. Source. Vickers.

enemy side. A few weeks later the magazine proudly showed a two page 'before and after' photo spread and the 'after' picture with their interpretations is most interesting. It has an English language commentary for the benefit of the Americans mostly, and it is carefully cut so that all the devastation created in the Woolston shopping and residential areas are omitted so that the myth that they only hit military or armament sites could be maintained. The comment reads, "Here again we present irrefutable testimony of the effect of German bombs in the shape of two photographs taken by German reconnaissance planes, showing a British armament factory at Southampton-Woolston before and after an air raid............ The photograph on the right plainly shows the devastation and havoc wrought by the German bomb raid (1) the shop has been hit and completely destroyed by fire (This was the Itchen works. Author.) A hole in the roof of the assembly shed (2) indicates the point of entry of a heavy bomb that doubtless did its duty in the interior. (This was the roof to Taggart and Morgans timber storage shed next to the Itchen works. It is plainly obvious from the picture that the bomb did not even explode. In the 'before' picture this timber store is said to be 'the machine shop'. Author.) "Sheds (5) and (6) have also been badly hit and are partly burned out, but the dwelling houses close by remain undamaged." End of partial quote.

As part of the Works ARP Control there were scattered around the factory site 'Consol' shelters made by the Nickel Co of Erdington, Birmingham, in which two volunteer 'firewatchers' would remain during a raid to report to the Central ARP which was located in the rising ground behind the paint shop on the opposite side of Hazel Road. We had one of these shelters in 'K' shop where I worked and the two lads of my age who manned it later confirmed for me from their own observations that the damage was as I have stated here and not like the German version, nor like some of the other tales that have been bandied about by persons who should have known better.

It is interesting that the German account says that the Itchen Works were completely destroyed by fire. This was not at all correct as from my own observations at a later date there was not the least evidence of fire, in fact, of all the raids on the works the only evidence of an attempt to create a fire was one 'camouflet' type

Aerial view of bomb damage to the Woolston factory after the raid on the 26th Sept. 1940. Vickers.

type bomb - this is what they called their oil filled bomb - which fell in the yard of the Woolston Works between the worksheds and design office block near to the river's edge and spilled its contents without igniting.

Even the bomb which struck the end of the design office block did not have the destructive power the Germans might have wished. It made a mess of the Chief Designer's office and flying glass and masonry penetrated a little further in to the building, but the bulk of its five storeys were intact and were used during the war mostly, I understand, as storage for various bits and pieces to do with the Pluto pipeline project and other items for the future invasion back into Europe, and after the war by an engineering firm and later by a firm making chicken plucking machines. It was finally demolished in the eighties. The Itchen Works was eventually rebuilt, mainly on its original iron skeleton, returned to Supermarines, and after they had withdrawn to South Marston passed on to other companies and remains today in shape and format much as it was in 1940. The archway that trapped the unfortunate staff was filled in when the ground beyond the railway embankment was brought up to the embankment's height after the war.

Itchen Works metal structure as it was left after dispersal. It was rebuilt after the war and re-inhabited by Vickers again when the Swift and Scimitars were built. Vickers.

It is one of those ironies of life that, as one of my colleagues said to me some years later, "Had one had the nerve perhaps the safest place to be during those raids would have been to stay in the factory."

The main Woolston Works were never rebuilt and the site was cleared in stages, but finally when the new Itchen River bridge was constructed.

It may be of interest to readers that a bound volume of some of 'Der Adler' issues - including the one to which I have referred - is available from the Public Library upon request.

At the conclusion of the Thursday afternoon raid the factory was sealed off by the Army and we were debarred from entering - possibly because at that time the existence of unexploded bombs could not be discounted. Later in the week parties were recruited to clear up and remove the jigs and tools that it was vital to save. A few, like myself, wangled our way in by showing our works passes to an amenable soldier to collect our own equipment.

Naturally the widespread dispersal that Beaverbrook demanded took time to organise and find suitable premises in Newbury, Salisbury, Reading, Trowbridge, and during this settling time the only real Spitfire production was dependent on the number already on final assembly at Eastleigh, and the transferring to Eastleigh those mainly finished wings and fuselages undamaged from Woolston and Itchen, and a certain amount of make-do had to be accepted which in many cases resulted in personnel being moved from temporary site to temporary site as the movement of tools and equipment took place. To quote my own experience I went to Hendy's Garage behind the Woolworth store in Southampton High Street, to Sewards Garage at Shirley, and then to Hendy's Agricultural Showroom at Chandlers Ford all between the 26th September and the 23rd October before being moved once more to Trowbridge in the following June. Many others experienced similar fluctuations; all at short notice. Transportation was chaotic until things had settled down, but somehow no-one seemed to mind - the circumstances and the larger issues of the war that had now been brought so close to home overrode any minor matters that in peacetime would have caused an uproar.

For some these new circumstances caused them to send their families away to what they thought might be safer places, the breadwinner remaining at home, and gradually almost all of us were obliged to go into lodgings as we progressively moved further from what had been our home base.

This brings me to one of the reasons for writing this postscript. The premier publication on the Spitfire is undoubtedly Morgan and Shacklady's massive tome 'Spitfire - The History', the results of so many years of research and giving, so far as their researches go, information on every Spitfire and Seafire built. Even to the most casual observer such a detailed and exhaustive enterprise must be prone to error, even when large chunks of it are taken from official Air Ministry records. The problems they faced in compilation must have been daunting and nothing I have to say about their book is intended to demean its wider overall value, but it is necessary to point out that here is a case where neither of the authors were at Supermarine at the relevant time and regrettably have fallen victims in some respect to, either persons who have given them information that they omitted to properly check, or have accepted as gospel the views of a few who were seeking to portray themselves as being in positions of greater influence than they deserve. Let me quote an example!

The book has various Appendices and the one on 'Production and Dispersal' is patently not written by either of the authors, but claims to be someone who was present at Woolston at the time. This account has some statements in that makes those of us who were present blush with embarrassment.

We were bombed, as I have just related, but in this gentleman's account he states "that sixty bombs struck the works at Itchen and eighty the Woolston factory, and that both factories were devastated".

The truth is, and this is still relatively easy to confirm from survivors and/or the local ARP reports, that <u>seven</u> bombs hit Woolston and only <u>one</u> penetrated the Itchen factory. The factories were not devastated, damaged a bit, yes, but not enough to prevent the management from getting most of the precious jigs and tools away intact to the comparative safety of the dispersal units. It will be seen in my autobiographical account that I, among many others, were actually back at work by the following Tuesday - some within the 'devastated' Woolston factory machine shop even earlier.

This only goes to show how careful one must be when reading or even watching programmes of wartime events on films or television.

The same book also tends to mislead in respect of the dispersal after the bombing; giving the main credit where it does not belong.

The clearest warning of the enemy's intent was the raid on the Cunliffe-Owen factory at Eastleigh in their belief that it was the flight hangar and final assembly centre for our Spitfire production.

Immediately Wilfred Elliot took steps to effect some kind of dispersal and members of staff, of whom George Guard is one still living, were sent out to find suitable locations. All they were seeking was large enough covered buildings with the requisite roof clearance to allow the erection of either wings or fuselage main jigs and of course a good concrete floor. The most obvious candidates were the larger garages and motor showrooms and as business in their normal activities had been severely affected by the wartime restrictions most of the ones approached were only too happy to allow their premises to be hired. Some were not so accommodating and where this occurred the Ministry of Aircraft Production Requisitioning Officer was used so that the site could be commandeered, but their intervention mainly happened after the bombing.

I have mentioned how I was moved from Hendy's Garage to Sewards Motors in the week following the bombing and both these sites had been taken over before the fateful 26th and in the former case, spare fuselage jigs were already in position. This is all that permitted some of us to recommence work by the weekend (or in my own case on the Tuesday). Sewards had been scheduled to become another fuselage assembly site, but the raids came too soon for this plan to be implemented and for a while it was used as a storage and sorting depot for tools and materials from the damaged Woolston factory.

The Hants and Dorset Bus garage in Winchester Road and the Sunlight Laundry were also acquired, the former for Wing building jigs and the latter for detail manufacture as its roof was not high enough to take the jigs. There was a little *contretemps* with the H & D garage as it had earlier been claimed as a storage depot for Southampton's ARP trailer pumps and sandbag stock. After some negotiation with the Town Clerk's office it was agreed that Spitfire wings were more important and that the Council's requirements could be easily found elsewhere.

The wider dispersal insisted on by Lord Beaverbrook only came into effect after the bombing, but the same means were applied by Wilfred Elliot to locate suitable sites with their centres located at Newbury, Reading, Trowbridge and Salisbury. The Works Engineer's department was able to offer guidance from their plans in respect of size and weight of equipment to be moved from their newly requisitioned office in the Southampton Polygon Hotel.

These dispersals naturally had a great affect on the original Woolston and Itchen employees and require a more detailed account of their own.

Although I have been able to draw on the recollections of some of my colleagues I am only able to comment with first hand knowledge on the two areas with which I was personally involved, but the reader may be reasonably sure that much of a similar nature took place in most of them. With that proviso I shall try to give an account of what I know, supplemented where possible with the comments of others in a later chapter.

Before leaving there are a few matters that need to be spoken of as they affect the future course of events.

The first concerns the Supermarine General Manager, Mr. Pratt, who came to us when Westbrook was returned to Weybridge. As I have mentioned, his style of management was distinctly different to that of Westbrook. I never saw him ever careering round the workshops and it appears he was content to allow Elliot, with his vast experience of those workshops and their personnel, to manage them, which he did, quietly and thoroughly. When Beaverbrook came on the scene in May 1940 he sent small teams of 'Investigators' to each of the major aircraft factories so that they could render to him daily reports of production and/or delays.

In the first instance the Supermarine allocated Investigators arrive without prior notice and Pratt refused them entry to the works. Personally, bearing in mind the security situation current at the time, I think he was quite justified in refusing entry until their bona-fides were established.

This little episode probably did not help in what later occurred. Beaverbrook's men, (one in particular who was a rather nasty piece of work) began to 'interview' senior executives of the works staff (not design) regarding their duties, staffs, etc., and determining whether or not the individuals were 'up to their jobs'. One such, on whom a negative return was made was Mr. Pratt, although what experience these interrogators had as a basis to make their judgements has always remained a mystery to me.

Nevertheless, it seems, according to an executive who was close to the centre of things at the time, as well as being interrogated himself, that the impression was given to Pratt that he was not performing as well as they expected. Pratt had had years with Vickers and was very closely associated with Barnes-Wallis prior to the construction of the successful airship R 100, which although it performed well was scrapped in the aftermath of the R 101 disaster. Sir Robert McLean obviously thought well of him when he sent him down to replace Westbrook in January 1937.

To compound this shadow over his future, Pratt was at Itchen Works on the Tuesday when it was bombed, and injured. This rendered him *hors-de-combat* for a while and in the interim James Bird (of more later) filled the temporary General Manager's position. Eventually he returned to his dispersal office at Hursley Park but became very depressed - after all he had managed very well from 1937 to 1940 - and Sir Charles Craven, then head of Vickers was endeavouring to find him a new position, but by this time Sir Charles too had been sucked into the Beaverbrook maul and the intentions lost in the hectic activity of those fateful days.

Sadly, although very little was said about it at the time, the depression got the upper hand and Mr. Pratt shot himself at home one afternoon after the Beaverbrook minions had had him removed from office.

Mr. Pratt was replaced by Squadron Commander James Bird, late of the Royal Naval Flying Service, and later still pilot for Supermarines Channel passenger air service, followed by a joint partnership with Hubert Scott-Paine in the ownership of Supermarines (the name comes from their telegraphic address) until the partnership was dissolved and James Bird bought out Scott-Paine's interest. It was thus that in 1928 James Bird sold his interests to Vickers, when he retired.

As soon as war was declared James Bird offered his services to the Supermarine - Vickers Company in whatever capacity they thought he might be of use and he was quickly put in charge of the Company's Civilian Repair organisation for Spitfires. Operating from a makeshift office in the Boardroom at the Woolston Works he guided that facet of the Company's work until Pratt was injured in the Tuesday raid when he took over the General Manager's functions until Pratt's return; and subsequently permanently after Pratt's dismissal. During the period after Pratt's return and his leaving, Bird shared an office at Hursley Park on the C.R.O. work which gives rise to a delightful sidelight to his character as told to me by one of the participants in this triangle.

There was, as might reasonably to be expected in the circumstances immediately following the bombing raid that prevented any further work at Woolston and Itchen, a degree of chaotic make-do in a variety of requisitioned premises, especially to the various office staffs. At first a floor of the Polygon Hotel was pressed into service by clearing its bedrooms of their normal furnishings, but that location had obvious disadvantages due to the strong possibility of further, more general, enemy action against the town, and eventually Lady Cooper's offer of Hursley Park, her home some eight miles out of Southampton, was accepted, the house becoming the Company's new Head Office, and shortly afterwards the Design Offices moved there from Southampton University premises into temporary buildings that were erected in the grounds.

A section of the gathering for a Sports Day for the Trowbridge Area. In the doorway from L to R is Charles Johns, Chief Inspector, Squadron Commander James Bird, the General Manager, and next Wilfred Elliot, Works Superintendent. Front centre, Vernon Hall, Area Manager, immediately behind him James Butler, Chief Production Engineer, and two from his left William Heaver, Area Manager of Salisbury units. Vickers.

Commander Bird's C.R.O. accommodation did not receive very much of a priority rating and upon Pratt's return to duty instead of 'pulling rank' as he might well have done, instead he walked into the office where Elliot's Secretary and his Personal Assistant were ensconced (a converted bedroom) and politely asked "if I might have a corner in your room for my desk," and there, with their consent, he worked until the call came for him to fill the General Manager's post again. That, to my mind, shows the true measure of the man.

He maintained the General Managership until the end of the war, often visiting the dispersal sites, even to the extent of attending some of their Sports Days and presenting prizes.

I like to remember him best as he stood just outside of the Woolston Works main gate whilst the rest of us were scurrying for shelter during a raid alarm, with his tin helmet on, the strap firmly in position under his strong chin, and his hands thrust into each of his side pockets with their thumbs protruding in a typical Naval stance, and a look on his face that said clearer than any words, "No bloody Jerry's going to move me!"

His services were justly rewarded with a knighthood after the war when he retired once again to his Estate at Wickham, where unfortunately a shotgun accident killed him whilst he was shooting in his grounds.

Tragedy seems to have dogged those who played important roles in the Spitfire's production. Trevor Westbrook fell foul of the internal politics at Weybridge having been rude to some highly influential Air Marshal and was summoned to the Company's Head Office which had been moved to Bath, where he was summarily dismissed. In fairness, it has to be said that his downfall there was of his own making, as he was reputed to be rude even to Sir Robert McLean, but he was fairly quickly snapped up by Beaverbrook for his Ministry of Aircraft Production team when it was formed. The sad side of this brilliant production engineer's life was an ill-fated marriage to an American divorcee, which also ended in divorce, and a solitary sort of existence in various well remunerated jobs - I recall seeing him at the Farnborough Air Show one year and he looked so lonely and forlorn to me that I plucked up enough courage to go and introduce myself to him and remind him of his Supermarine days, but he still struck me then as a 'loner', - and in the end, whilst out walking one cold evening he had a stroke and lay all night in a ditch in freezing conditions near his home in Lurgashall near Pulborough, and died.

Another, who is remembered, is Jim Butler who filled the posts of Production Manager and Chief Estimator from way back in the thirties until late 1941 or '42. In that role he was responsible to Westbrook and Pratt for the Planning, Ratefixing, Tool Design, and Estimating which in his timespan dealt with the then new metal construction of flying boats - Scapa, Stranraer, Seagull, Walrus and Sea Otter - but also the first gull-winged fighter which was fortunately unsuccessful and allowed the prototype and subsequent production of Spitfires and ultimately Mitchell's Bomber project. A truly awesome spread for his limited number of staff, which I can well appreciate having held similar positions in my later years. Jim Butler was not tall, but slim with a thin face and a small military style moustache and his hair brushed straight back no doubt to cover its diminishing amount. With his work load I am not surprised that his rare visits to the shop floors were short and swift.

When the works were bombed his car suffered a certain amount of panel damage to bonnet and wing, but not sufficient to prevent its use. When the move to Hursley was made it almost coincided with the move of the panel-beating section to the requisitioned agricultural showroom of Hendy's at Chandlers Ford and Butler arranged to have our squad repair this damage, and this task was carried out by Jack Rolf and myself in the last week in March 1941 according to the bonus card entry in my notebook.

Unhappily, Butler was slowly going blind, and not all that long afterwards we heard that he had to give up his work. Another sad end.

So with Commander Bird and Wilfred Elliot at the helm, so to speak, the production of Spitfires from Supermarines began its new fragmented life in dispersal units after its main works had been put out of commission through enemy action.

At this stage of my narrative I would like to draw the reader's attention to the first of the contributions from Denis Webb's memoirs which, although confirming a lot of what has gone before will add to the account because it is viewed from a management angle and details items and events which I would personally have been unaware. So that the full flavour of his account is not lost I am reproducing it word for word how he has sent this part of his manuscript to me. It is headed as follows:

The Long Expected Chop

On Sunday evening 15th September 1940 I had just got home from the Works when the Air Raid Warning was sounded and we heard explosions in the general direction of Woolston and soon saw clouds of smoke rising and I guessed that the Jerries were having a crack at the Works. The All Clear sounded soon after and I though I had better get back to see if I could help Pratt at all as Wilf Elliot was up in Castle Bromwich.

When I got back to the Works there was no sign of serious damage although a host of windows had been broken and Gerry Gingell and the Works Fire Brigade were busy clearing the remains of broken glass from the windows of the bridge across Hazel Road from the Works to the premises across the road.

Pratt was on the 'phone and Tom Barby, the nightshift foreman, was checking over the main buildings to see if a nightshift could be run as it was about 6.30 pm by this time. I don't think there was any doubt that it had been a deliberate attempt at hitting the Works and not just a hit and run affair on the town but the only damage done of a serious nature was to the homes of the people living near the Works where there had been quite a number of casualties.

In all probability Pratt had telephoned Sir Charles Craven to tell him of the events as they were old working colleagues and kept each other informed. We used to get fairly frequent assessments of the state of the war in the air and I will always remember on one day, Pratt, on seeing Elliot, said "They reckon it will be all right now." It seemed a very optimistic remark to make considering the general state of affairs, but it was made one evening after the biggest daylight battles had taken place in the air and we had survived. This survival on our part had meant that Hitler had to call off his invasion plans and so give us a chance to build up our strength again.

Tom Barby and Pratt had decided that it would be impossible to make the Works 'light tight' by the time it was dark and so the nightshift was cancelled. Quite a number of the men had moved out to the New Forest and Bournemouth with their families and those of the nightshift had got themselves organised very well with a motor coach to bring them in every night. On this night they arrived just after we had decided that the nightshift was impossible and some of them made it very clear to me that they thought we ought to have got ourselves organised better and 'phoned them before they left Bournemouth and so saved a wasted journey!! There were a few occasions when some of us wondered if the war was worth winning.?

I think it was the next morning that two of Beaverbrook's boys arrived apparently without any credentials or authorisation or identity papers to announce to Pratt that they were here to disperse the factory! In view of all the warnings we had had against saboteurs and such like, Pratt, apparently and correctly in my opinion, refused them entry to the Works until their identity could be established. But the correct action did not endear him to the Beaverbrook crowd and, I think, had tragic consequences.

Elliot arrived back from Castle Bromwich and it was decided to requisition some premises in Southampton and prepare them for occupation while further preparatory work was done in Hendy's Garage, in Pound Tree Lane, and Sewards Garage in Winchester Road. I was sent to see the Manager of the Sunlight Laundry in Winchester Road which was on the outskirts of Southampton and to tell him we were about to requisition his Works and ask him to move out as quickly as possible. I don't remember any great opposition although rather naturally the idea wasn't popular but they, I think, decided to merge with Liners Laundry in Millbrook and soon began to move all their machinery out.

My next task was to go and see the Deputy Town Clerk who name was Bernard Fishwick, and ask him to shift all the Trailer Pumps of the Fire Brigade out of the Hants and Dorset Bus Garage in Winchester Road where they were housed and protected by massive enclosures of sandbags. This was the only building in the area with sufficient clear height to take the Spitfire wing jigs.

He refused on the basis that the Fire Brigade Trailer pumps were of more importance to the town than bloody Spitfires. My argument that bloody Spitfires in adequate numbers could made trailer pumps unnecessary was not accepted so I said the matter would be referred to Beaverbrook and Company who would undoubtedly enforce their removal and we parted.

Someone told me that there was a row of empty huts not far from Hollybrook Cemetery which might be useful for a Finished Part Store Headquarters and I had a look at them and agreed. Lowther's Garage in Shirley had also been earmarked and was taken over as a possible machine shop. So all that week we were busy getting the old occupiers out and making preparatory arrangements for us to move in if necessary. I went to a local builder in Winchester Road and got him to build a brick passageway to link up all the huts at Hollybrook Stores so that at night there could be free movement between the buildings without having to have light traps on the doors. While in the builders office drawing up plans, a woman clerk started to complain that with Supermarine in Winchester Road they would get bombed now! I said "Well Woolston has had most of it up to now and surely in wartime we should share and share alike!" As I left the office I said some rude words about the female, who turned out to be the builders wife! Never a dull moment!?

I think that Sunlight Laundry got all their stuff out by the weekend, but we found that the roof trusses were absolutely deep in cotton lint which was festooned everywhere, giving me the answer as to why nothing lasted long when sent to the laundry! It took us quite a while to get it all cleared off as we didn't want that mixed up with our sub-assemblies.

The deputy Town Clerk had had to submit to having the Bus Garage counter-requisitioned from the Fire Services and had removed his trailer pumps by the weekend, but all the sandbags were still there and we were trying to find out from him where we could dump them - it being anatomically impossible to put them where we would have liked.

While at lunch in the Mess at Woolston on Tuesday 24th September the bofors around the works started firing like mad and things whistled down. Everyone immediately dived for the door to get to ground level and a safer place as fast as they could. I was hurtling down the stairs and passing the apprentices lecture room when I realised I still had a glass of beer in my hand and hastily darted into the lecture room and left it on a desk, thinking there was enough glass around without me carrying some with me. I rushed on down and into the materials test room which was slightly below ground level with nice thick walls. On the way I vaguely noticed faces peering anxiously from the doors and windows of the Erecting Shop and the Works Police were milling around wondering whether or not to sound the warning.

I think it was eventually sounded, but by that time the raiders had gone and as gunfire and other unpleasant noises had ceased I joined Elliot , whom I found by the ARP Headquarters and he told me there had been a lot of damage at the Itchen Works.

We got up there and found that a stick of bombs had apparently fallen across the shelters causing a lot of casualties, especially as one of the bombs had fallen near the tunnel under the railway through which everyone had to go to reach the shelters. A mobile First Aid Post converted from a single decker bus was soon on the scene and our own First Aid and Rescue people were at work Elliot suggested that I scramble over the railway embankment to see if there was anything I could do and when I did so I could see the full tragedy. The bombs had missed the target (the Works) as usual and instead had landed on some of the shelters, which in one case had turned into a heap of soil and sand with arms and legs sticking out. Rescuers were already frantically digging in the hope that some people might still be alive.

I came across two young men standing absolutely still and just staring as if turned to stone. I said to them "You had better get into one of the shelters until the All Clear goes", but they were oblivious to everything and it dawned on me that they were in a complete state of shock. I took them by their arms and said " You had better come with me away from here" and they reacted slowly and went with me as I guided them back to the First Aid Post and shelter at the main Works, where I handed them over to the medical people.

My doctor, Dr. Brierly from Dibden Purlieu, when I told him about this much later, said that one of our men who lived in Dibden had run to the floating bridge and from there to the Hythe Ferry and from Hythe to Dibden and had been taken to him for treatment and had remembered nothing of the whole episode.

Shortly after I had taken the men to the First Aid Post the Warning went again and I remember the horrible feeling of claustrophobia when huddled in there, with thirty or more frightened people as we felt the near misses shake the ground and dirt fell from the ceiling. I think that general panic wasn't far away but a Works Policeman, an ex-service chap, started singing a hymn, which everyone gradually took up.   I am pretty sure no one was singing from any religious feeling but it distracted the mind, released some nervous energy and calmed everyone down.

After the All Clear we went on trying to help the injured and one instance sticks in my mind.   A lorry came down from the Itchen Works and stopped outside the Shelter and First Aid Post and I saw Hatley, a young chap from the Planning Department sitting on the side of it. He was calling out 'Any more for the mortuary waggon" in a calm voice as if this was his normal occupation. We all saw then that the floor of the lorry was covered with corpses, few showing any sign of injury - just killed by blast.   In spite of everything a burst of laughter rang out as one of the 'corpses' suddenly struggled to sit up yelling "I'm not dead - its my bloody leg that's broken!" So we gently hauled him onto a stretcher and into the First Aid Room.

There were a considerable number of casualties that day, I believe over a hundred killed and numerous injured.   I remember that Mrs. Pratt was one of those who volunteered to go round and break the news to the relatives.

However, it could had been considerably worse if the Warning had sounded before the raid started and the bombs had caught thousands as they tried to reach those shelters.

Thinking about it all afterwards, I could not help wondering if some of those killed had lost their lives because we had moved the fuselage jigs to Itchen in order to make things safer for them. Even at Itchen it became clear that if the workforce had stayed in the Works and not run for the shelters they would all have survived.

On Wednesday I was at Itchen Works early in the morning with Arthur Nelson looking at the mess and pondering where to start, when someone came up behind us and put an arm round each of our shoulders and said "Good morning Nelson - good morning Webb - it looks a mess, but don't worry - you'll sort it out alright!" We looked round and found our cheerful companion was Sir Charles Craven, who had apparently driven down from London to see how things stood for himself.

He asked after Pratt and we had to tell him he was off sick, probably at the Hospital, as he had been blown from one side of the embankment to the other, injuring his hand in the process and probably suffering from shock. After a few more words he went off to find him, leaving me for one completely astonished that the Chairman of Vickers-Armstrongs, who at that time had such heavy responsibilities, should not only find time to visit, but also that he should know my name.

After Sir Charles had left us, Arthur Nelson and I had a further look around and came to the conclusion that the best thing to do was to get the Finish Part Store, with all the parts that would be used at Hendy's Pound Tree Lane and Sewards, out of the Itchen Finished Part Stores and moved over to the Hollybrook Stores, and this was started in an orderly manner.

Later when I saw Elliot, I mentioned the occasion and he also said that Sir Charles was a remarkable man. Elliot continued, "If he ever asks you questions about anything, be absolutely sure that you answer truthfully - don't try to pull any fast ones, or you will be caught out"

I asked jokingly, "You speak from experience?" "Yes" said Elliot, "I do". I think Elliot's experience with Sir Charles - which he related - left him with a profound respect and admiration for him.

There must be something about the Navy which makes marvellous administrators and leaders of men like Sir Charles Craven and Squadron Commander James Bird.

I was busy trying to get people and things sorted out along Winchester Road on the 26th September, when the Germans came over again to put the finishing touches to their Tuesday's work. One could hear the pounding going on quite clearly and was thankful that we had got so many men and so much material out in the interval, although there was an enormous amount still to be shifted. I got into my car and drove over to Woolston to see what was left, but as I got near the sirens went again and I halted near a pub close to the floating bridge which kept the lids to its cellars open in any air raid, so that anyone could dive in. A direct hit would probably mean death by drowning in beer - could one ask for more?

While I was contemplating making use of the cellars, I saw one of those hilarious occurrences which always seemed to take place in moments of tension. One of our lorries and a bunch of labourers had started to clear rubble from the road to the Works when the siren sounded. The labourers promptly leapt into the lorry, which immediately accelerated towards the main road where I was standing. On turning into it, in order to go up Portsmouth Road in the direction of the open country, the driver took the corner too close and a wheel dropped into the rather deep gutter. This shook one of the labourers off the tailboard and as he fell into the road I recognised 'Yorky", an elderly, grizzly bear of a man, with the huge thick boots of his calling, who was reputed to be a bit simple and slow on the uptake. The lorry didn't stop and I saw this great hefty fellow pick himself up and pursue the lorry with an acceleration and speed which I would have considered quite impossible - he caught the lorry at the crossroads about 50 yards up the hill!

Clearly the driver and everyone, including Yorky, considered that the neighbourhood of the Works was to be left at all costs, and who can blame them after experiencing this second raid.

The 'All Clear' sounded soon after and I went in search of Wilf Elliot, who I found undamaged and talking to Wing Commander

Kellett, our RAF Overseer.   Both were understandably taking it in
turns to imbibe from Kellett's flask!

I think I should mention here Elliot's usual place during an Air
Raid if he was at Supermarines. We had a shelter built close to
the entrance to the offices and this was reserved for handicapped
employees, such as those partially crippled or wearing leg-irons,
etc. and Wilf Elliot used to sit in the entrance to this shelter during a raid, giving a running commentary as one might do at a
football match.   He would comment "I can see another one coming, yes he's dropped one and I can see it falling, but it will miss by
miles. There's another, silly bugger's overshot with that one, " and
so on, and it must have been a great comfort to those less mobile
of our workforce, as there is nothing worse than being cooped up
and not knowing what was happening, even when you are a fit
person This act was typical of the man.

Again little serious damage was done as far as the work in progress
was concerned, although the fuselage of the projected bomber was
damaged, but that had been held up by the Ministry anyway, but
the damage to the buildings and the adjacent houses in which
many of our men lived was appalling.

My immediate concern was for the Finished Part Stores. Those at
Woolston were still undamaged, but up at Itchen a "near miss"
had caused a wall of the stores to collapse and a storage bin had
fallen more or less into the crater. However, one of the storemen
reported next day that they had managed to save virtually all the
parts. We had been moving the stores from Itchen to Hollybrook
with a certain degree of method, but after this further narrow
squeak I decided to take rather drastic steps and told the storemen
to get everything out into a lorry and to take it to Hollybrook and
tip it out on the floor of one of the empty buildings, then send
someone to Hendy's and Sewards to tell the foreman and
chargehands that they should send their operators to Hollybrook
to pick out the parts they normally assembled in order to keep
them going while we moved the bins and got everything back to
normal. Rose (Finished Parts Supervisor) was in the meantime
battling away to get all the Woolston stuff moved, but the parts at
Itchen were the ones, a shortage of which would immediately affect the flow of fuselages to Eastleigh.

Casualties in this second raid were not so heavy as in the first. We lost 37 killed in the Works and some 52 others outside the Works, such as nightshift men in their homes, as well as a few who had fled from the site. This was amazing considering the magnitude of the raid and was probably due to the warning being sounded a bit earlier, which gave people a chance to disperse. I saw Fred Amey and Ted Gregson soon after and they said that they had bolted up the road to Peartree Green, an open space with public shelters, and they added they had been assisted into the shelters by a blast!

Jim Weedy, the Foreman of the Wing Assembly shop, started for the Green, but things got so bad that he dived under a Brewer's lorry which was standing outside the pub at the bottom of the lane which ran up to the Green, thinking it would give him some protection. He lay there, endeavouring to claw himself down into the road and then put his arms over his head and prayed hard! Unknown to Jim, the lorry driver had decided to make a run for it and had leapt into his cab and driven off and with all the noise of bombs exploding and bofors firing, Jim had never heard or felt the lorry depart!

In due course the noise all died down and Jim cautiously opened his eyes and looked around to find he was lying in the open! Poor old Jim! He was able to laugh at the incident afterwards, but that experience, plus the appalling damage done all around where he lived finally broke him and he never returned to the Works, although he came to see us at the Polygon on one occasion and I was shocked by his appearance. He recovered finally and the last I hard of him he was working for Imperial Airways.

The Thursday raid really put "paid" to any idea of using the Woolston or Itchen Works again. This then was the end of the Supermarine Works at Woolston, but we had done our job, producing every possible Spitfire until Castle Bromwich got into full production.

The Minister of Aircraft Production (Lord Beaverbrook) visited the Works in the evening and ordered complete dispersal and evacuation of the works.

I shudder to think what would have happened if the Luftwaffe had carried out those raids in the Spring of 1940, or during the "phoney war" period.

It was rather a sad business collecting all the stuff out of Elliot's office and my old office after all the years spent there, but on the other hand I felt an enormous sense of relief that the long expected chop had come and I had survived, although sadly so many others had not. Nevertheless, what Pratt and I had so often worried about had not occurred - no one had been killed in any panic rush, and no bombs had fallen on the thousands as they streamed up the road to the Itchen shelters.

We were at last free to get to Hell out of it! In the process of doing just that we became less polite about everything, and those bloody sandbags in the Hants and Dorset bus garage were bulldozed into the Tramways Depot at Portswood. At that stage we had no proper organisation for deciding on layouts and installation of machine tools or equipment and so simply transported benches and equipment of a shop to be moved and let the foreman decide how best to see the place in which he found himself.

Syd Bloxham, who had been with me at Hythe on 'Stranraers' during what now felt like a previous existence, sorted things out at Sunlight, as that dispersal unit became known for the rest of the war. I remember someone bewailing the fact that the electricity supply wouldn't work our equipment, being a different voltage or phase or something. By the time I had relayed this to Elliot and returned, one of our electricians had borrowed, stolen, or otherwise acquired, the necessary gear to make it all work. It appeared to have been the case of our man knowing someone in the Corporation Electricity Department who knew where the necessary gear could be found and everyone using their initiative.

I think there were numerous cases such as that, where someone had the initiative to improvise and a determination not to be beaten by the situation and so enable progress to be made while major moves were sorted out.

Rose, of the Finished Part Stores, worked with a will to get all the thousands of parts out of Woolston Store with the bins and records and install the lot in Hollybrook. Some of the men were very disheartened and felt that they would never get it sorted out. I pointed out that it was no worse than the original sort out - the Stores had been in a bloody mess then but we had managed to get it all shipshape and with that practice we should find it easier this time! They gradually cheered up, especially when they woke up to the fact that they no longer worked in a prime target area! After Woolston, Hollybrook Stores and Winchester Road felt a million miles from the war. (Note. Denis Webb had been charged by Trevor Westbrook to reorganise the then existing Supermarine Finished Part Stores at Woolston in the middle thirties, a task which I personally can vouch he carried out most successfully. C.R.R.)

I found that being anywhere in either Woolston or Itchen Works, or rather the remains of them, filled me with profound unease and an intense desire to get away from the place as soon as possible. It was completely irrational, as with both places out of action there was little likelihood of the Jerries paying them any further attention, but a curious smell and aura hung around the place - a sort of witches brew made up of violence, fear and death. The irrationality of the feeling was emphasised by the fact that an equally intense feeling of relief appeared if one went just as far as Peartree Green which was only a few hundred yards away! I felt thoroughly ashamed of this fear until I found that many others had it as well. Pratt talked openly about it and weeks after the raid he disliked being anywhere near the Works and his wife had experienced the same thing. Both agreed it was a totally irrational feeling, but very real. (Note. It will be remembered that Mr Pratt had been caught at the Itchen Works in the Tuesday bombing and had, in fact, been blown right over the railway embankment and suffered some injury. C.R.R.) I never found out what Elliot felt. He being small and rotund seemed to have the resilience of a rubber ball to which he had a close resemblance. Whatever happened he seemed to bounce back unchanged.

According to Andrew and Morgan's book (Supermarine Aircraft since 1914) the first raid on the 24th September was carried out by 17 Messerschmitt Bf 110 bombers, one of which was shot down. Six near misses blew most of the roofing off the Works and one bomb was a direct hit on the shelters.

In the second raid, on the 26th, the Germans sent 55 Dornier D.O. 17's and 10 Heinkel HE 111's with a fighter escort of Messerschmitt Bf 109's and 110's. One Heinkel and two Messerschmitt's were shot down for the loss of four Hurricanes and two Spitfires. They dropped 70 tons of bombs in a single carpet bombing attack.

I believe, but do not know for certain, that our fighter boys were fooled by the Jerries in as much as the Jerry fighters came in first and when our fighter boys appeared the Jerries went out over the New Forest and so drew our fighters after them, thus clearing the way for a run by the German bombers.

* * * * * * * * * * * * * * * * * * * *

That concludes Denis Webb's particular chapter, which to my mind is important for the reason that, so far as I can establish, he and I are the only two persons who have written in depth on these raids from a personal involvement, especially in respect of the Tuesday raid when we both went to the scene of the actual bombing and assisted as best we could with the rescue work. He also has taken note of the account that was in Andrew and Morgan's book and supplied by Ian James. The differences and discrepancies of this account, as in so many others who were not present at the time, is apparent from Denis's chapter and my own Spitfire Odyssey published in 1985.

Before leaving the matter of the bombing I would like to include, for the reader's benefit, an account of my researches into the one particular German Luftwaffe Squadron, Erprobungsgruppe 210, that was specifically charged to destroy Spitfire factories in the Southampton area. Time has erased the heat and hate held during those tragic days, but there was another side - the enemies - which can now be incorporated as a counterweight to our losses, even if they do not balance out.

Chapter Three - Erprobungsgruppe 210

Although unaware of it at the time, the raid on the Spitfire Works on the 24th September had been carried out by the same German squadron that had made the raid on Cunliffe-Owen's and the one that had so damaged Woolston on Sunday September 15th, namely Erprobungsgruppe 210, and subsequent postwar research enables me to give some details of this particular 'crack' squadron.

The Luftwaffe High Command had realised by the middle of 1940 that their 'Stuka' JU 87 dive-bomber was not going to be as effective in the air war upon which they were now embarked as it had been when acting in the role for which it was designed as a close support aircraft for their advancing armies. Our fighters found them very vulnerable, especially as they came out of their dives, and the casualties began to get unacceptably high during their attacks on shipping in the Channel and more so once they commenced operating over southern England within easy reach of our defending fighter squadrons.

The idea was created for the use of fighter aircraft equipped with a small bomb load to utilise their speed and defensive capabilities to attack specialised targets and then fight their way out. It was some little time later that the R.A.F. caught on to this and followed suit.

The 'Experimental Group' 210, to anglicise the German nomenclature, was formed at Rechlin by a dynamic Swiss born German named Walter Rubensdorffer using only ME 109 and ME 110 type aircraft fitted with under wing or fuselage bomb racks enabling them to carry varying bomb loads depending on the target distance and consequent fuel loading. Obviously the nearer target would be preferable and once they could operate from the captured French airfields this greatly facilitated their task. Most of the time they used Denain, just south of Paris as their base, but with typical ingenuity landed at the closer airfields around Calais or Cherbourg as satellite springboards for final topping up prior to making the Channel crossing.

At first they operated, with some success, against shipping in the Channel, but when the Luftwaffe's attack was shifted to endeavouring to beat the R.A.F. their skills were required for more advantageous targets to that end.

Erprobungsgruppe 210 were embarked on a short, not entirely unsuccessful, but bloody career in cost to its own members. Enemies they may have been, but with the passage of time and its healing properties over the feelings of hate and danger engendered fifty years ago, one can only admire the courage this small band of airmen brought to their cause.

To appreciate it one has to give the broad canvas against which they worked. In June the British Forces had been expelled from France with the 'miracle' of Dunkirk salvaging most of the men whilst losing all of their arms and equipment. Lord Dowding had courageously hung on to his rapidly dwindling fighter aircraft force by impressing upon his political masters (much to their distaste at the time for which they never forgave him and later ignominiously retired him) the illogicality of throwing away the aircraft we were going to need to survive in the already lost battle of France.

Once the elation from their continental victory had subsided plans were put into operation for the 'Master Race' to invade the British Isles to subdue this last enemy on Hitler's western flank before he turned against the Russians. The story of how the invasion barges built up in the Dutch, Belgian and French harbours is well known and much of the personal tale that I have related thus far has taken place with the events of defeat in France, Dunkirk and the Invasion threat being its backcloth. That the Invasion did not take place is to the eternal credit of the R.A.F. Fighter Command under the inspired genius of Lord Dowding's leadership and the courage and dedication of the men and women of his Command. The odds against him were stupendous - the thought of losing too terrible to contemplate.

At first the Luftwaffe carried out probing raids across the whole of the British Isles aided by the shortened distances now available from their newly conquered bases before embarking on their main pre-invasion task of eliminating the R.A.F. That was essential to landing their forces without incurring unacceptable losses.

Erpro: 210 commenced its operations from Denain airfield and tried out its tactics first against shipping in the Channel. (Most of the foregoing information has been gleaned from Francis Mason's 'Battle over Britain': still to my mind the best reference book on the subject, and to whom I gladly acknowledge my debt.) The first date that Erpro: 210 was deployed is not clear, but references to them appear early in July 1940 when a ME bf 109E is recorded as 'crashed and burnt out, cause unknown' at an unidentified airfield in France on July 8th and on the 13th one ME bf 110 'crash landing at St. Omer after damage from A/A fire over Margate.' The pace quickened noticeably after July 16th following Hitler issuing his infamous Directive No. 16, which said roughly "that as England refused to come to terms with our hopeless military situation he intended to eliminate us as a base operating against Germany and if necessary occupy the country completely." The Battle of Britain had commenced!

Raids were directed against the south coast areas, some of which I have already referred to when they involved Southampton, and up the East coast. Erpro: 210 appears next when another of its ME 110's was shot down near Harwich on the 25th and a raid it was making on a convoy of ships in the Channel on the 29th was intercepted by Hurricane fighters and damaged before it was driven back to its base at St. Omer. Another was shot into the sea when two ME 110's appeared near a convoy off Suffolk. From both the latter raid and the Harwich one it is significant that one member of the two-seater 110 was saved in each. In both instances it seems as though the rear gunners were picked off first and then the R.A.F. fighters went for the engines.

On August 1st thirty HE 111's of another Gruppe attacked the Boulton-Paul factory at Norwich inflicting damage and casualties, but a later follow up attack on the same target by Erpro: 210 on the 10th August was defeated by the bad weather conditions prevailing at the time. Two more Erpro 110's crashed at their Denain airfield on August 4th killing one crew member in each case. The greatest loss to date to be suffered by Erpro 210 occurred at Denain again when their ME 109 squadron (Staffeln) leader Valesi was killed through an accident. Erpro: 210 was made up of three 'squadrons', two using ME 110's and the other ME 109's. Valesi was a very experienced pilot in the type of attacks they were developing.

By this time in the overall development of the battle the Germans were beginning to use the great armadas of bombers escorted by dozens of fighter aircraft restrained by an edict from Goering to stay with the bombers, thus losing them their tactical advantages. In their particular configuration Erpro: 210 as a Gruppe would comprise of 3 or 4 Staffeln of between 10 and 12 aircraft each, depending on serviceability, with a few additional aircraft allocated to staff duties. As we know that their composition was 2 Staffeln of ME 110's and 1 Staffeln of ME 109's it would appear at most - even with a fourth Staffeln of which there appears to be no record - their total complement was about 50 aircraft. Losing Valesi, one of only 3 Staffeln leaders on August 7th, was only the beginning of a very tragic turnover of leaders in a relatively short period of time.

On Sunday 11th August a party of Erpro; 210's ME 109's led by their commander Rubensdorffer himself mounted an early morning raid to shoot down the balloon barrage at Dover followed by 17 of the bombed up ME 110's who dropped approximately 60 small bombs without causing much damage. The number of bombs relative to the number of aircraft indicates that they possessed a variable in their bomb racking, as broadly at that time the Germans were using mostly 50, 100, 250 and 500 kilogram bombs. (1 kilo = 2.2 lbs.) Later that same morning, before midday, Rubensdorffer mounted another attack with other bombers on a convoy off the Clacton coast during which 2 of his 110's were shot down, one each to a Hurricane and a Spitfire.

On Monday 12th August Erpro: 210 made pinpoint attacks on the radar installations along the south coast. Leading 4 sections of 4 aircraft each they peeled off in sections, Oblt Otto Hintze attacking the Dover installation, Wilhelm Rossiger's section aimed at Rye, Martin Lutz went for Pevensey and Rubensdorffer's section for the radar unit near Faversham in Kent. The latter station 'remained on the air' and at the other three locations they were only off for about six hours. Nevertheless this limited triumph encouraged the German Commander Kesselring to launch an attack 'through the hole' on two small Channel convoys, then later a much heavier raid on Portsmouth, whilst simultaneously a group of 15 Junker 88's turned off and swept down on the Ventnor radar station striking the site with a concentration of 15 500 kg bombs with great effect.

Rubensdorffer's Erpro: 210 however, had not done yet and by 1 pm they were involved in a ferocious low level attack against the Manston airfield. Right on the cliff's edge their approach near to water level and then powering up and over the cliff edge caught the defences by surprise as they screamed across with all their guns blazing and bombs dropping, whilst almost simultaneously other German bombers rained down their loads on the stricken airfield creating further havoc. Of the few Spitfires that managed to get airborne as the raid was in progress was none other than Supermarine's Test Pilot Jeffrey Quill who was on detachment to No: 65 Squadron for operational experience. Only one of Rubensdorffer's 110's was shot down that day.

As we now know the raids of the 12th were the prelude to 'Eagle Day' on the following day when Goering commenced his all out attempts to crush the R.A.F.'s fighter forces and secure for his 'Leader' the control of the skies essential for the success of their invasion plans.

On the 14th Rubensdorffer led his two Staffeln of ME 110's in another devastating attack on Manston creating further mayhem, but this time losing two of his aircraft to ground defences.

The next day, to be remembered by R.A.F. personnel as 'Black Thursday', was to see some of the most ferocious air battles ever fought. The weather was none too clear for August which was a disadvantage to both air forces, although we did have the inestimable benefits from radar in positioning our aircraft for interception. There is at least one book devoted solely to the air fighting of this one day, but we are concerned only with the fortunes of Erpro: 210. After lunch, pockets of clear weather made operations possible and 210 mounted a full scale attack on Martlesham aerodrome with its ME 110's whilst the 109's attacking a nearby Signals site. The damage at Martlesham was sufficient to render it inoperable for 48 hours. Freed from their bombs the 109's took on attacking R.A.F. fighters, shooting down three Hurricanes, and all returning to base without loss, as did the 110's. This was probably the Gruppe's finest achievement as retribution was about to overtake them.

The 15th of August will be remembered for many reasons, the ferocity of the air attacks on airfields, factories and civilians alike, and the first real emergence of the massed formations of German aircraft which were to become such a familiar sight over the southern towns and countryside in the ensuing months, but it was a relatively small raid that cast a longer shadow than was apparent at the time.

By early evening Rubensdorffer was airborne again from one of the French airfields with eight of his 109's and fifteen 110's. He should have joined with a batch of Dornier bombers scheduled to attack Biggin Hill R.A.F. station, the two formations covered by an upper layer of Messerschmitt 109 fighters, but as so often in the heat of battle conditions prevailing that day things did not go according to plan and he missed his rendezvous with the escort, and realising the Dorniers would have to face the defences alone he decided to make his targeted attack on Kenley by sweeping round to the north, bomb Kenley from that direction then head towards Biggin Hill to provide fighter cover from the Dorniers. Having swept round over Sevenoaks he commenced a diving run from the north that should bring him directly over Kenley and sighting an aerodrome coming into his line of flight sped in and attacked it with bombs and gunfire causing considerable damage. Unfortunately it was Croydon airport - not Kenley.

The importance of this error lies in the fact that Hitler in his Directive No. 1 on 'The Conduct of the War' as early as August 31st 1939 had specifically stated re bombing "The decision regarding attacks on London is reserved to me." Croydon came within the boundary of London!

Rubensdorffer however was unaware of his mistake and had more than enough to worry about as moments before his attack a squadron of Hurricanes had scrambled from that very airfield and had just time to turn and catch the Germans as they were leaving the scene of destruction they had created. Splitting their formation into two or three sections (presumably on orders by radio from Rubensdorffer) they endeavoured to seek the shelter of what cloud was available, but Squadron Leader John Thompson, with three companions from 111 Squadron, latched on to the section led by

Rubensdorffer himself and in the running battle that followed Thompson shot down one 110 whilst other squadron members shot down a further four more and one 109. Thompson's day was crowned however by catching Rubensdorffer and shooting him down in flames near Rotherfield. Thus from the twenty three aircraft that had set out that evening, by half past seven, seven had been destroyed, and apart from losing their leader, Erpro had lost two other Staff members including the Staffeln Adjutant.

Perhaps it was as well that Rubensdorffer perished in battle as it is almost certain he would have incurred the unpredictable fury of Hitler for contravening his order, and more so when as a result of this raid on the Greater London area instigated a reprisal raid on Berlin on the orders of the Cabinet. This raid, on the night of 25/ 26th August, in turn led the German Leader to commence his 'blitz' on the city from September 7th thus diverting a large portion of his bombing strength in relatively fruitless tactical raids on the civil population when it might well have served his purpose better to have proceeded with the plan to grind down the R.A.F.

It was five days later before Erpro: 210 put in another appearance, this time under its new leader, Hauptmann Von Boltenstern, in another attack on Martlesham which mainly failed to hit the target and distributed its bomb load outside of the airfield's perimeter for the loss of a ME 110 and crew killed from a Spitfire attack. On the 22nd August Erpro: 210 made one raid on a Channel convoy under heavy fighter cover and later on the same day another raid on Manston with escorting fighter cover and without loss.

Meanwhile, the damage already being done by the raid on Croydon, the German Leader cancelled his instructions not to bomb London until he said so and consequently on the night of the 24th August over one hundred bombers made their ways to the capital after 11 pm to attack, almost without hindrance, the Thames dock areas that were clearly defined by the twists in the river's shape.

No doubt some reorganising was required after the failure of the last Martlesham raid to achieve the high expectations that had arisen during Rubensdorffer's leadership and August ran to its final day with only two more ME 109's crashing on their airfields and injuring their pilots, but on the 31st they returned to the fight by bombing the Radar installations in Kent and Sussex putting them out of action for the day. Later, about 5.30 pm, they combined with other bomber units in raids on the airfields at Hornchurch and Biggin Hill which resulted in their losing another aircraft being shot down and a further two crash landing back at their aerodrome.

Oblt Otto Hintze, Staffel Leader of the section of ME 109's which bombed the Cunliffe-Owen factory. He was later shot down and survived the war as a prisoner. Source. John Vasco.

They turn up again on September 4th making a feint raid on the radar at Poling to disguise the main attack intended for the Hawker Hurricane plant at Weybridge (which hit the Vickers Works there instead) in the course of which their new commander, Boltenstern, was shot down and killed with his crew member near Tangmere. They returned with other bombers and fighter cover to attack the Hawker factory on the 6th, but failed to inflict any more to the production hindrance to this Weybridge unit incurring the loss of another ME 110 and its crew from that excursion.

September 7th, the Luftwaffe commenced its day and night attacks on the city of London and massed formations of bombers and fighters became a truly awesome sight in which Erpro: 210 played its part by creating diversionary raids as evidenced by one of its 109's being shot down between Portsmouth and Southampton by A/A fire and the pilot captured unhurt. Another 109 was damaged in a takeoff accident on the 8th September.

Messerschmitt ME 109 similar to the type used as a fighter-bomber by Erprobungsgruppe 210. Valentine & Sons.

By now Martin Lutz had been appointed Gruppe Commander following Von Boltenstern's death and was tasked with eliminating the Spitfire Works at Southampton. The long awaited Invasion had been expected to materialise with the favourable tides and after the heavy raids on the 7th, and the alert code word 'Cromwell' was dispatched at seven minutes past seven that evening, but mid-morning on the 8th a reconnaissance Spitfire (ironically K 9787, the very first production Spitfire from the Eastleigh Works and Southampton factories) was able to establish through the adverse weather conditions that no barges or landing craft had put to sea. Later we found that the Invasion had been scheduled for the 7th but with the weather being unfavourable for paratroops, plus the Luftwaffe failure to gain control of the skies, it had been postponed until the 21st.

Erpro 210 Gruppe Leader Martin Lutz who led the Woolston raids of Sept. 15th and 24th. He was killed a few days later over Cranborne Chase. Source. John Vasco.

The German Messerschmitt ME 110 also used as a fighter-bomber. Valentine & Sons.

In the interim, Oblt Otto Hintze leading the 109 Staffeln of Erpro: 210 had carried out the raid on the Cunliffe-Owen factory on the 11th September as described earlier.

Fortunately Otto Hintze survived the war after being shot down and captured at the end of October. He has provided personally accounts of 210 to Peter Townsend and another author who I met when he was researching for a book he proposed on this extraordinary Luftwaffe squadron, both sources from which I have extracted that which is pertinent to my story.

Having 'blooded' his 109's Martin Lutz was no doubt keen to similarly give his 110's the chance to show their mettle and this resulted in the raid intended for the Woolston Spitfire works that I have described for Sunday 15th September. According to Francis Mason's research eighteen ME 110's took part and there is no record of them suffering any losses. As we have seen however the raid failed to achieve its target objective.

Having been established at a new base on the Cherbourg peninsula from which the raid of the 15th had come, Martin Lutz now prepared for a pin point attack on the Spitfire Works once more. Making a direct run from his base to the Works with eighteen of his ME 110 bombers and covered overhead by fighters from another squadron, Martin Lutz led them straight on to the target despite the heavy defensive A/A fire with the results that I have detailed earlier for Tuesday, September 24th. How frustrating it must have been to all the Luftwaffe Command to see from their reconnaissance photographs that the factory was still undamaged one can only guess. For Martin Lutz it was his last fling at us, for three days later he led his Gruppe once more in an attack on a Bristol aircraft factory in concert with others which found the British fighters waiting for them. They pressed home their attack and reached their target but in the running fights that followed, Martin Lutz was shot down and killed in Cranborne Chase. Three other 110's were shot down in the same raid, one killing the Staffelkapitan Wilhelm Rossiger. It was only from a prisoner from one of these aircraft that the true dimension of the Erpro's activities came to the attention of the British authorities. They had lost three Gruppencommanders and four Staffelkapitane in six weeks with correspondingly high losses among the crews in the same period and yet by all accounts their morale and fighting abilities were unimpaired.

On Wednesday the 25th September, 210 was out again in an attack on Portland - very often a favourite target for the Luftwaffe during its invasion preparation phase - acting as a diversion from the main raid on the Bristol aircraft works at Filton which caused heavy casualties, and is extremely well accounted in Ken Wakefield's book 'Luftwaffe Encore'. That same evening they made a further raid; this time on Plymouth. Throughout the day's activities they do not appear to have suffered any more losses.

So far as I can fathom from the information I have been able to gather there seems to be no record of their participation in raids on the 26th and they appear to have been resting for a day prior to the Friday raid which ended so disastrously for Martin Lutz.

September passed into history and it is not until Saturday 5th October that Erpro: 210 once again re-grouped under a new commander, Werner Weimann, and with eighteen of their 110's operating from a fresh base at the Pas de Calais, made one of their specialist attacks on West Malling airfield. Unfortunately they ran smack into 303 Polish Squadron Hurricanes, and although they were able to inflict some damage and casualties it was paid for by the loss of Weimann and another aircraft with two further aircraft damaged in crash landings back at their base.

Bad weather diminished the raiding in the early days of October and it was along this time that the Luftwaffe, taking due note of the achievements of Erpro: 210, introduced more 109's equipped with a bomb carrying capacity with which they were able to carry out single aircraft attacks over a wide area in 'sneak raids' (or Jabo's) taking advantage of the weather and cloud conditions as they existed.

A raid on Kenley airfield at 8 pm is believed to have been carried out by 210 in which four Hurricanes were damaged on the ground on the 15th October and a 110 was damaged in a landing accident at St. Leger in circumstances unknown on the 21st October, but it is not until Tuesday 29th October that Erpro: 210 reappears in its old aggressive role: this time with a dive bombing attack on the

North Weald airfield and the ME 109's this time bombed up with 3,100 kg bombs each and under the command of Oblt Otto Hintze. According to reports this raid was carried out with the brilliance that one would have anticipated from a leader of Otto's experience and it caught a number of our aircraft in the process of taking off, causing two Hurricanes to crash, killing one of the pilots. The remaining Hurricanes, once aloft, gave chase and were fortunate enough to shoot down no other than Otto Hintze himself. He managed to bale out and was taken prisoner.

Otto Hintze, who had taken part in most of Erpro: 210's ME 109 raids, including leading the one on Cunliffe-Owens, and the ill-fated Croydon raid, was probably at that time the Gruppes most senior and experienced pilot, and recognition of his services was acknowledged by the award of the Knights Cross 'in absentia' a month later. Martin Lutz was awarded the same honour, but in his case it was posthumously.

October 29th cost the Gruppe another ME 110 which crashed whilst taking off in France killing both of its crew.

So far as I can establish the Gruppe's final raid took place against Ipswich on November 17th. Under the command of its latest, and last, commander Hptm. Von Ahrenhein, it made a sharp attack with its 110's bombing whilst its 109's acted as top cover. It is believed the unit was disbanded later that same month.

The records show that in its short, glorious, if bloody, five months existence it had lost fifty crew members killed and four taken prisoner of war, twenty six ME 110's and four ME 109's.

Chapter Four - A Personal View of Dispersal

As I mentioned earlier I can really only give an authoritative account of the Beaverbrook dispersals from my own experiences, but here and there I am able to insert information that has been given to me since by others which I feel able to incorporate because, in my opinion, they can be relied on.

When I left the Spitfire 'in jig' rear fuselage plating job I moved to the panel beating and Wheeling squad under its leading hand Jack Rolf.

It took a little time until I could contribute satisfactorily to production as that particular aspect of the trade I had chosen required adapting to the peculiarities of the skills and for a while I was only given Walrus panels to shape, but once the Walrus work was off-loaded all five of us 'wheelers', Jack Rolf, 'Mac' Mutten, Charlie Chapman and Hilton Duxbury, concentrated on forming skin plating for Spitfires, aided also by Fred Waygood who did some of the 'bashing' jobs like cockpit coaming channels which twisted and turned at odd angles. For a long time we were the sole suppliers of many of the fuselage skins, most importantly the top rear one which in the early days defied any attempts to press it successfully as it had an awkward reverse curve where it joined the upward sweep that led to the fin. Another panel that only Jack Rolf could make successfully was the front nose fillet panels, so it can be readily understood why this squad had to be reconstituted as urgently as possible after the bombing so as not to imperil their delivery of vital parts. There were also many other sections of the works that required equally urgent reassembly, but this is the one that I am most familiar with and will serve as a guide to the others.

Imagine if you will the problem. With the exception of a few who were recognised early and recruited into the tasks of clearing the factory of the essential jigs for fuselages and wings, removing to Eastleigh the undamaged, or lightly damaged fuselages in their advanced assembly stage at Itchen, and all the other design and commercial equipment and paperwork, so necessary in the running of the whole enterprise, no one knew at first who was even alive from the two raids. When we approached the works on the

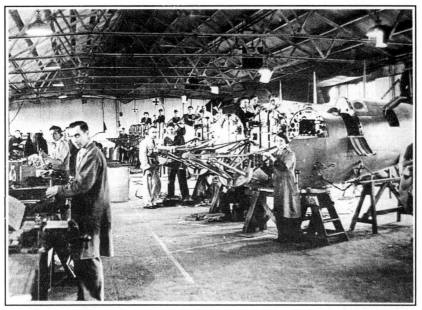

The top floor of Seward Motors where a dispersal assembly line was established. Vickers

Friday morning we were told to report to the local Labour Exchange and it was from there I received my instructions to report to Hendy's Motor Showrooms at the rear of Woolworth's store in the centre of Southampton where I reverted back to the skinning operations under Bill Peckham our 'K' shop foreman on the Tuesday, but on the following Thursday I was told to report to Sewards Garage in Winchester Road where our Wheeling machines had been deposited with mounds of other bits and pieces from which we gradually located our original benches and other equipment necessary to continue producing the panels. The raw material stores were being dumped elsewhere and sometimes we were delayed for supplies and the amount of space we required was severely curtailed as other equipment and tooling arrived from the bombed works until we were virtually working at the entrance door at the top of the ramp as the growing quantity of rescued bits and pieces pushed us further out. This problem was solved when we received instructions to report to Hendy's Agricultural Equipment showrooms at Chandlers Ford which had been requisitioned (after some argument) on the 22nd October 1940.

This sort of gradual migration and sorting carried on for some months, the units being formed in the immediate proximity to Southampton being the first to recommence production despite the travelling, feeding and other problems as the almost daily air raid alarms came and went in the prelude to the major night attacks that started in November.

Our travel arrangements for just the five 'wheelers' was by Jack Rolf's car except for Hilton Duxbury who had removed his family earlier to his hometown up north and he took lodgings in Chandlers Ford. For food we made an arrangement with the adjacent Hut Hotel to provide us with cooked lunches. For a while we were the sole occupants of the Showrooms then after a short while the odd racks of finished parts began appearing and also a couple of near completed wings.

As the floorspace became increasingly occupied and then an office was built within and the Stores Manager with his secretary installed it became obvious that our tenure was likely to be short lived.

Unfortunately that did not occur until the following June and before that the 'blitz' hit Southampton. Travelling back and forth in Rolf's car had to be tailored to suit the blackout requirements, (there was none at first in the showroom) and the almost clockwork precision of the evening siren howling heralding the possibility of being caught out in a raid.

For those workmates in the Southampton dispersal units it was even worse, as they were on the receiving end of some small, but sharp, bombing attacks. One nasty one on the 5th November 1940 hit one corner of the Civic Centre, barely a hundred yards from the Polygon Hotel where our office staff had first been located, and it killed a number of school children who were there for art classes. Although we could not work a nightshift at Chandlers Ford the Southampton units had been blacked out and so the night attacks increased they were in the unenviable position of having to go to local shelters near to the units whilst their families had to fend for themselves at their homes.

November 17th brought the first of the worst night raids to the town when parachute mines were dropped and caused widespread damage, especially to the lower end of Manor Road in Woolston where a whole area of residential properties bounded by Manor Road, Bond Road, Mortimer Road and Radstock Road were virtually flattened. But that was just the foretaste of worse to follow.

It seemed, and still seems, that for some reason the Luftwaffe chose weekends to bomb Southampton. The parachute mine raid was a Sunday, and the next weekend, on the 23rd we had the first of the major attacks.

According to the invaluable volumes of 'Blitz - Then and Now' a 'major' attack is where over one hundred tonnes of high explosive bombs are aimed at the target. In their table of bombs aimed in night attacks between August 12th 1940 to June 26th 1941 Southampton comes seventh with a total of nine hundred and seventy one tons of high explosive and an additional eighty eight tonnes of incendiaries from what they list as seven 'significant' attacks of which four are termed 'major'. A significant attack is where approximately fifty tonnes of high explosive are aimed at the target.

The major attack on the 23rd November was followed the next weekend with one on each of the Saturday and Sunday nights and so caught many of us at home, or in my case at the girl's home in Peartree who I was courting at the time.

The story of the Southampton 'Blitz' has been told quite adequately in Tony Brode's book 'The Southampton Blitz' and in greater detail with lots more pictures in 'Southampton at War' by Antony Kemp. I have also given some of my recollections in 'Spitfire Odyssey', but did not elaborate on the general theme. No one who experienced the blitz, in whatever town or city, will forget the awfulness of having to sit it out for sometimes as long as thirteen hours as the bombers droned over with their peculiar desynchronised engines, the crash and bang of the anti-aircraft guns, the whistle and crump of exploding bombs (particularly the 'zip' which was all you got for the one close to you) and the curious rattle of descending incendiaries released from their containers as they fell, and then to emerge to see the fires and damage caused. On Sunday the 1st December 1940 I travelled right across Southampton by cycle to seek out members of my Mother's family, one at Mount Pleasant and the other at Redbridge. I was appalled by the devastation in the town where the emergency services were still operating - the town centre had been gutted by both bomb and fire and hosepipes littered the roads; ambulances still shuttled back and forth with the casualties still being recovered and often too late to save. The two families I sought were fortunately unhurt, and only minor damage to their homes, but my Aunt at Redbridge on learning that I was working at Chandlers Ford gave me a note of introduction to a relative who ran the Conservative Club there requesting their help in giving me lodgings so that I would be saved the daily journeying and the nightly perils. When I returned home I told my parents and they begged me to go, so somewhat reluctantly I took their advice and so missed the Sunday night raid which only added to the misery of the remaining Sotonians.

It was not until I made this residential change that I realised that hundreds were 'trekking' nightly, often on foot, sometimes by cycles, and some by organised coach parties, into the countryside around Southampton to find a night's shelter as best they could. At the Club I went to they were even sleeping under the billiard tables or in the coach that had brought them on the Club's forecourt. In the morning they would pack up their few possessions and trek back: some to find their homes gone, others thankful that theirs were safe so that the husband and sons could return to their daily tasks.

It was an awful period, and I often think of Southampton High Street and the destruction there, the complete destruction of Edwin Jones store in Houndwell (where once I had worked as a boy), and the many homes in various states of demolition when I hear that the Germans are kicking up a fuss over the bombing of Dresden. It would be well for them to remember that he who sows the wind reaps the whirlwind.

Supermarines unit behind Woolworth's shop had to be vacated for a while as the adjoining wall between them had collapsed and production had to be abandoned for repairs. One of the areas at the Woolston Works that had escaped any serious damage had been the main stores at the Floating Bridge end of Hazel Road and as the priority in dispersing was on jigs and machinery the removal of stores was left and one of the night raids hit it causing the loss of a considerable amount of equally vital, but thankfully in time replaceable, parts and materials.

Apart from the raids I have mentioned there was a continuous loss of valuable production time in the Southampton area dispersals by the many smaller, but none the less dangerous, raids that occurred almost daily or nightly. Anyone who studies the Luftwaffe's bombing campaign will find that although they mounted major attacks against many of our towns and cities they almost always used smaller striking forces to carry out simultaneous diversion raids on widely dispersed targets all over the country. Of these, because they were so conveniently to hand, Southampton, Portsmouth and Bristol, were favourite often allowing the German bomber crews to make two trips to the same site per night.

Because of this, the need to adopt the wider spread dispersal units received the urgency it required and although the overall plan was to develop each area as a self-contained Spitfire producing area, complete with its own airfield, this was not achieved until much later.

Trowbridge, like all the others, had to originally make do with requisitioned premises, like garages and a steamroller factory, until the beginning of 1942 when the Hilperton factory was purpose built and then later Bradley Road's much larger unit eventually enabled wing and fuselage assembly, but it was not until late summer of 1943 that they were provided with a purpose built hangar erected alongside the airfield created for the R.A.F. from farmland at Keevil, five miles away, that they had the facility to finally assemble and test fly their area's production.

Salisbury was luckier, and whilst wings and fuselage etc. were made in requisitioned bus garages and motor showrooms the local Wiltshire Flying Club's airfield was available for assembly and flight, as was another suitable flying field created from the horse racing gallops at Chattis Hill near Stockbridge. A certain amount of transporting was required but the ubiquitous 'Queen Mary's' coped with that.

Eastleigh, much to everyone's amazement seemed to bear a charmed life. Having failed in their attempt of September 11th

The Barnes Steamroller factory at Southwick, Trowbridge where the Wing Leading Edge build was sited. Note the partially assembled leading edges outside beside the steam rollers

raid to destroy the Spitfire Flight hangars when they struck Cunliffe-Owen's instead, the old World War One American built hangars survived this second was intact and continued to produce Spitfires for their final assembly and flight stages longer than any other unit, even into the post war era when a number of Spitfires were purchased off the Ministry for refurbishing and sale on to a variety of foreign governments, and some converted to two-seaters for a training role. When I first left the Company on the 8th July 1947 one of my last jobs was to finish wheeling to shape a set of engine cowling side panels.

Reverting to the dispersal story, and mainly staying with the course that affected me, which is very broadly as it affected the majority of my colleagues, by May 1941 it has been decided that the panel beating and wheeling squad, now increased by two more members and located all together in the one site at Chandlers Ford should be broken into smaller segments and dispersed. Jack Rolf was intended to lead one section to Trowbridge comprising Charlie Chapman, Fred Veal, and myself, whilst Hilton Duxbury went to Newbury, Mac Mutten remained in one of the Southampton units with Ron Gerry. Gerry and Veal were the two additions to the original 1939 squad.

My move was delayed by a day or two due to my presence being required at an inquest, but soon after I joined the others in the ex-steamroller factory at Southwick on the outskirts of Trowbridge Jack Rolf managed to arrange his own transfer back to Southampton on compassionate grounds and I found myself left in charge of the section.

Southwick was primarily a unit devoted to the production of the wing leading edge assemblies and we were allocated a corner of one of their sheds.

Prior to leaving Chandlers Ford I had left my first lodgings in the club as it was obvious to me that my hours of work and theirs were not compatible and I accepted an offer to move in with Hilton Duxbury which helped our landlady to cope financially after her husband had been called up for military service. During that period, having got the agricultural showroom blacked out the two of us used to work on until eight o'clock, often through the raid alerts which we felt safe enough as we were those valuable six miles distance from Southampton. We were lucky, although some bombs fell in Chandlers Ford and far too many lumps of anti-aircraft shell pieces clattered down nearby, we kept the extra hours of production going on some of those essential panels. After our relocations I never saw Hilton again, although I have recently learned that he ended his wartime days at the Shaw Works at Newbury as Chargehand of the press section there. I'm afraid he was only the first of the many old colleagues that I never met again.

I kept the wheeling squad at Southwick going despite Charlie returning to Southampton (again a compassionate posting) with just Fred Veal and myself, a young lad I was allowed to engage as our general labourer until the October when I was moved for other work at the Fore Street garage in Trowbridge itself. There I was given a squad of ten or so to make an air duct required for the Photographic Reconnaissance Spitfires that were being developed.

Fred and I shared 'digs' in Trowbridge with the family of a railway engine driver. Practically all of the Southampton personnel trans-

Rutland Garage, Trowbridge which became a coppersmiths shop. Vickers.

Fore Street Garage, Trowbridge requisitioned to become a Detail manufacturing site and until Bradley Road was the Area Head Office.   Vickers.

ferred to create the 'hard core' on which to expand the production employees with men and women who were being drafted into the aircraft industry from all over the country had to be found accommodation - mostly 'digs' - by the local government Billeting Officer who had the unenviable task of ordering people to take in boarders if they had rooms to spare.

This very often meant that the boarders were there on sufferance, but I must add, that so far as I was concerned I had very little to complain about. The Billeting Officer's name was Gilbert Wortt and much later, in 1944, I found him to be an excellent tennis player.

Trowbridge at that time only had - for Spitfire production - Fore Street garage, which was mainly bench fitting work with some welding and, as I found, a very useful Greek cabinet maker for making hardwood tools; Rutland Garage in Bradley Road where a section of the coppersmiths from the Weston (Southampton) unit had been transferred, and the steamroller factory at Southwick making wing leading edges. There was a stores unit in nearby Westbury run by Johnny Coffin. The Area was under the control of Vernon Hall an ex 'F' shop man with Leslie Brown as his deputy and they were housed in some small offices within Fore Street garages.

The importance of the scale and contribution made by either newly recruited labour and those drafted in from as far apart as London, Bristol, down to Devon, and a good handful of escapees from the Channel Islands needs to be acknowledged here. The overall picture reveals that from roughly 1500 people employed at Southampton and Eastleigh in 1939, this figure ended the war at something like 10,000, of which 60% were female. It was quite incredible to witness how these many and diverse types of individuals buckled down and took over many of the jobs that at one time were considered exclusively the province of skilled men.

Day and night shifts alike they shared the same primitive conditions that prevailed in the early days of dispersal with few complaints, although it was obvious to some that the whole business of being away from their homes, living in hostels or lodgings and working closely with men, had been a cultural shock.

A word of praise is also due to those on whom we were billeted in all the Unit Areas. It must have been very inconvenient to suddenly find you had to share your home with someone you did not know and whose style of living might be vastly different to your own, in habits, religion and other various ways. The weekly bath - bearing in mind we were all restricted to the 'infamous five inches' of water - was a particular difficulty in homes where there was no bathroom and the tin bath had to be set down, mostly in the kitchen as I recall, and hand filled with water from the copper.

Sometimes moves could be arranged whereby lodgings would be changed if it was to the benefit of the three parties involved without letting the Billeting Officer know. I made three such changes during my first posting to Trowbridge without incurring the wrath of Mr Wortt who usually adopted a rather severe view of such liberties.

The Air Duct job came to a close at the end of January 1942 and for a time I worked at the newly built Hilperton Road factory - the first of the Ministry of Aircraft Production's purpose built plants in that Area and although it was very cold there in winter the work was not in my usual tradesman's capacity, but drawing up the layout plans for the benches and the pipe runs to supply each bench with electrical and pneumatic services that it would require once the employees from Fore Street garage moved in. Although this was only a 'fill-in' job pending a move to Salisbury it was to prove a very useful experience which came in handy many years later when I was working for British European Airways at Northolt, which to my mind goes to show that stepping outside of ones own trade category is not a bad thing.

The transfer to Salisbury emphasised this very point as it provided me with valuable experience at the flight end of production. My new post was at the High Post airfield about three miles north of Salisbury and the work in the tiny flight shed involved the reception of the equipped fuselages and wings, helping to assemble these two together - all done manually by most of the men there who would be summoned by the shout "All under the Wings" from Jack Draper the foreman once they had been trolleyed off the Queen Mary low-loader and the fuselage safely set up and tied down on

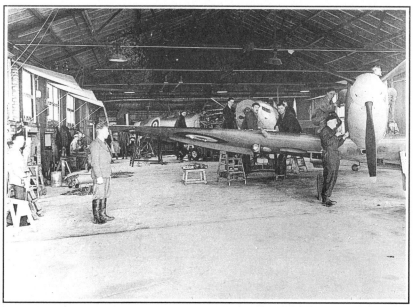

Although supplied as a photgraph of High Post the author believes it is really some of Chattis Hill, part of the Salisbury Area's dispersals. Source Vickers/CUL.

its supporting trestles. Eight to ten of us would take the weight of the wing on our backs on its under surface and shuffle our way into position as directed until the alignment with the fuselage wing spar had been made thus allowing the wing pins to be driven home. Considering the weight and awkward handling positions it was a marvel that no one received any personal injuries.

Once these main components were secured the various teams would descend on the aircraft to connect up the systems that flowed from fuselage to wings, i.e. control wires, hydraulics to undercarriage, pneumatics to gun bays, and electrics. When these were checked and passed by the Inspector, the next job was to function the undercarriage and as soon as that was cleared the wheels would be locked down and with the front supporting trestle removed the Spitfire stood for the first time on its own wheels and by removing the rear trestle support so that it settled down on its tailwheel the aircraft became manoeuvrable within the confines of the tiny hangar - it only contained three Spitfires and that required them to be carefully positioned - by two or three hands.

At this stage virtually the whole of the differing types of trades would come into play so that cycle time in the hangar was reduced to the minimum. The fillet support tee sections with their nutplates would be fitted by a girl on each side who would then continue with the actual fillet panels to close the gaps, top and bottom surfaces between wings and fuselage, with the exception of the nose fillets that were fitted by the sheet metal workers. Of these, the port side nose fillet bay required that a jig be fitted first to set the location of the camera gun mounting and from this jig the shape, size and position of the aperture for the camera gun decided, and the fixing of a door for access to the camera bay.

With the filleting completed, and this included drilling to allow certain drain pipes to emerge to atmosphere, the next major item was the fitting of the engine cowling panels which had been delivered in their sub-assembled, and rivetted state, but with surplus materials to their peripheries to allow for cutting in to suit the butt jointing positions with one another and the nose fillets and fuselage at frame five bulkhead.

Meanwhile the armoury team would be fitting and connecting up the eight machine guns, or four machine guns and two cannons, or alternatively just four cannons - depending on which armament and mark of aircraft each was scheduled to have. The Armoury was one room off from the hangar space and no larger than a reasonable dining room, but the guns were delivered there in their boxes and required some fairly hefty greasing removed before they could be inspected, checked that their mechanisms were easy acting prior to actual fitment into the wings. They would then be aligned by their concentric housings and connected to the ammunition boxes and linkage units with the facility for discharging spent cartridge cases. Whilst this was going on the painter would be touching up the camouflage paintwork where the joints of wing to fuselage had been made and applying his stencils to spray on the serial number that had been allocated to the aircraft.

As these operations neared their completion among the last would be the fitment of the propeller and the streamlining spinner and with the propeller set into a 'Y' position so that it just cleared the hangar door opening the now complete Spitfire would be pushed outside for the fuel tanks to be filled, various checks made, and then the engine run carried out by the resident Rolls-Royce representative. It was always a thrill to hear the cough and see the smoke burst out of the exhausts as the engine burst into life on the beginning of its fateful journey into the wartime unknown. Two of the hangar staff as well as the Inspector generally stood by as the engine test run was carried out. Sometimes, but not very often, some minor adjustments might have to be made and normally this stage of creation went very smoothly, but if necessary one of our gang would be on hand to remove a cowling panel or do whatever the R.R. rep. thought was required.

Once it was cleared for functioning the aircraft would be moved away from the hangar's proximity so that a compass setting operation could be done without the metal mass of the hangar interfering with the reading. Compass deviation cards would be marked with the appropriate entries and placed into the card holder that was inside the cockpit on the instrument dashboard for the pilot's information.

A final general look over by Inspection and the A.I.D. (Air Ministry representative) and if all was well the Air Ministry man would sign the documentation that authorised that the aircraft was ready for flight testing. The information would be passed along by telephone to wherever our pool of test pilots were operating from and soon we would observe an aircraft overhead, banking to check how our windsock was showing the wind's direction, then making its landing on the undulating surface of the grassy field to pull up near the hangar and disembark the pilot.

Most often the pilot would be a R.A.F. pilot seconded to testing Spitfires whilst 'on rest' from operational flying; in some instances he might well be either French, Polish or Belgian, but whatever his nationality he would have had operational experience in Spitfires and very often in the Battle of Britain. Sometimes we would get Jeffrey Quill himself - our Company's chief test pilot and it was always an experience to see this very expert pilot carry out his test flying - not with any unnecessary aerobatics for display purposes, but smoothly and accurately so that every flying facet and characteristic of that particular aircraft was examined and either found correct or it would be brought in and have whatever adjustments were required to meet the high standard he set.

Most frequently he would insist that the trailing edge of the ailerons should be dressed up or down so that the aircraft did not fly with a tendency for it to fly one wing lower than the other in level flight with the controls centralised. By this time (1942) the Spitfire had metal ailerons and one of the tinbashers would hold a supporting metal block under the trailing edge of the offending side and gently, but firmly, use a mallet to bend the last half inch of the edge slightly down; a move that would change the airflow just that little bit extra so that it lifted that side wing.

Not all flights were without more serious snags. The one which I remember in particular, as I happened to be one of the men on flight attendance duty for that aircraft, was following a flight of exceptional aerobatics by its Belgian pilot he casually mentioned that during some of his rolls he thought he detected some minor aberration in the port wing. When pressed by our Inspector he declared it to be "like something loose". I was asked by the Inspector to remove the fillet panel at the nose so that he could get his flashlight inside to have a look. It was as well he did, as just inside was a riveters 'dolly' bar about one foot long and an inch square of iron which had been thrown about inside during the high jinks the Belgian had so obviously enjoyed. Fortunately further inspection revealed that no other serious damage had occurred and the aircraft was passed for service use. Had that bar not been trapped in the leading edge forward of the main spar I'd hate to think of what the consequences might have been had it been loose where it could well have locked the aileron controls and caused a crash.

As soon as the new Spitfire had passed all its tests and the test pilot had given his signature, the A.I.D. would complete his Air Ministry form that officially took the aircraft 'on charge' and arrangements would immediately follow to have it flown to a R.A.F. Maintenance Unit for eventual issue to a Service squadron.

These delivery flights were most often carried out by members of the Air Transport Auxiliary Service which was mostly staffed by women pilots.

That they performed their wartime duties is generally recognised as beyond praise. I have personally seen them fly a number of different types of aircraft, whether single, twin or four engined, and only once did I witness an accident and that was not the fault of the young lady pilot who took corrective action and made a beautiful one wheel landing with a Spitfire and walked away as unruffled as though nothing untoward had happened. In my book they are heroines, every one!

The output from High Post was severely restricted by the hangar size and although we worked night and day shifts, month and month about, it was virtually impossible to increase our output, or indeed without the usage of Chattis Hill to absorb all the production emanating from the Salisbury units in the City. We produced on average, about six completed Spitfires a week, which in the circumstances was pretty good.

It might interest the reader to know how long some of the tasks I have mentioned actually took and how many bonus hours we received at one and fourpence halfpenny per hour (old money the equivalent of roughly 7p at today's conversion) so that some idea of our pay may be assessed. I can of course, only refer to the entries made at the time in my war notebook.

The operation descriptions and time <u>allowed</u> is as follows:-

Fit 'tee' bars at joints of nose and bottom fillets.   3 hrs per A/C
Fit and fix top and bottom nose fillet panels.   60   "
Fit and fix Camera mounting (Port side only)   11   "
Cut in and fix Camera Access door in fillet.   6 1/2   "
Fit and trim top, and both side Cowling panels.   12 1/2   "
Fit and fix Air Intake Fairing on fuselage.   12 1/2   "

It can be safely assumed that once the familiarisation stage had been overcome the 'actual times' taken were almost always one third of the above times. As there was only two tinbashers on either day or night shift at a time it will be seen that one pair would not clear a complete set of operations in a shift so that much of our work resulted in either starting on a fresh aircraft arrival or completing the previous shift's work on an earlier one.

From what documentation I have and more that has been un-

Anna Valley Motors, Salisbury, taken over for Spitfire building. Until the purpose buil;t factories were built adjacent to the Old Sarum Rings. This was the Area Head Office.   Vickers

The Wilts and Dorset bus garage used to fit out fuselages from the Wessex Motor's unit in New Street, Salisbury and build wings.   Vickers.

earthed it is apparent that of all the dispersal units intended to be entirely self sufficient (or very nearly) Salisbury is the one that got its act together first.

Wessex garage became the equivalent of the old Supermarine 'K' shop building fuselages, Anna Valley Motors in Castle Street took on the Leading Edge assembly and various other sub-assemblies, whilst across the road, in the requisitioned Wilts and Dorset bus garage, it was large enough to build the wings in and out of jig stages, as well as the installation work into the fuselages previously carried out at the Itchen factory. They did so well that they were able to keep both High Post and Chattis Hill airfields supplied with the main essentials for final erection and flights.

The only facet of manufacture that I do not recall in any great measure was a machine shop, and I gather that most of the units were similarly being supplied from the Newbury Hungerford, and later the newly built Shaw Works, and from Shorts Garage in Southampton. For a time the leading edges produced at Trowbridge (in fact all Trowbridge production initially was sent to other areas for use as they had no airfield or facilities big enough to accommodate the main jigging required for either wings or fuselages) were fed into Salisbury and the Hants and Dorset bus garage in Southampton where these assemblies could be managed. Consequently, for a long time Spitfires emanated from either Eastleigh, High Post or Chattis Hill airfields. From my researches it seems that High Post delivered their first Spitfire X4497, a photographic development type, for its first flight on the 12th January 1941 and Chattis Hill flew the fighter version R7250 on 18th March 1941. After that they seem to run neck and neck with their deliveries, each averaging six per week.

It must also be remembered that the Southampton Area under Arthur Nelson produced more aircraft than either of these two units using Eastleigh aerodrome which bore such a charmed existence considering its location to the major targets of the Luftwaffe, or Worthy Down to which the experimental flying had been relocated. It was not until near the end of 1942 that the dispersed Supermarine units and areas reached the heady totals of production that had been reached prior to the bombing, but of course by then the shadow factory was in full flow, of which more later.

My personal stay at Salisbury was very enlightening for experiences that were to provide well for me in the later years in the industry.

In the July of 1942 I was suddenly required to report to the Wessex garage down in New Street, Salisbury, right at the time when the 'Baedker' air raids were becoming a feature of the Luftwaffe's attention. The garage was not a decent stones throw from the famous Cathedral, one of the intended targets, but apart from a couple of alarms with few bombs that were far enough for us to ignore on the city, the change proved beneficial to me in more ways than one. Here at Wessex were mainly men from my old Woolston shop, the foreman, Charles Whettleton, having been Bill Heaver's riveting chargehand in 'K' shop, and they were engaged not only on the familiar fuselage building but the introduction of the alterations that were being called for to make a Spitfire into a Seafire for aircraft carriers.

This involved fitting at various stages of the fuselage build catapult fittings and hook assemblies, both jobs quite new to me, and involving with the catapult spool fitment a degree of accuracy that was unknown in the sheetmetal worker's world where plus or minus thirty thousandths of an inch was the order of the day; now we were required to fit these new attachments to within one and a half thousandths of an inch which had to be proven to the inspectors by 'blueing in' and feeler gauges. It was really a fitters job, but there were none about at that time so the sheetmetal workers buckled down and carried it out quite successfully. There is an old factory saying that a fitter is just a sheetmetal worker with his brains bashed out. Unkind, but in those circumstances and in factory parlance, much used however untrue. The fitting of the catapult gear I have dealt with in some detail in my 'Spitfire Odyssey' so I don't think it needs repeating here, other than to say it was an interesting experience.

My sojourn at the Wessex garage lasted until the March of the following year and during my time there I was able to increase my experience by other work than just the catapult fittings. When required I found myself allocated a variety of work that had not formed a part of the Woolston days. On checking my notebook for this period I find that I fitted brackets for Drop Tanks, Arrester Hook Fairings, Cockpit Coamings, Doors and Windscreens, and the sliding hoods. Sub-assemblies of the frames 6 to 10 with their longerons and bottom skins, and cutting the aperture and fitting the tail parachute container bay just in front of the frame 19 transport break, all added to the general knowledge of the fuselage build and some of the changes in design that came with the tail parachute anti-spin requirement and of course the adaptation for use on aircraft carriers.

When the fuselages had reached the desired stage of manufacture that could be dealt with in the Wessex garage it would be transferred to the Wilts and Dorset bus garage where the tail empennage which had been made further along the road in another unit - would be fitted and the engine support structure added. These additions permitted the fitment of much of the control cables and pulleys as well as the Merlin engines and the host of auxiliary equipment that the front face of frame 5 bulkhead provided an anchoring base, then the nose ring diaphragm that surrounded the engine's propeller shaft thus allowing the fitment of the square tube sections with their retainers for the eventual fitting of the cowlings at the aerodrome. The fuselage petrol tanks would be installed and as much of the fuel, hydraulic, pneumatic and electrical systems possible without the wings on. This Bus garage played a big part in Salisbury's contribution to production, as apart from the near completion of the fuselages it also built the wings, both in their jig stage and followed to as full a fitment of systems, including the undercarriage and wheels that enabled those at High Post and Chattis Hill airfields to keep their workload to just the minimum necessary for a rapid completion as well as consideration for the limited space they had.

The Anna Valley Motors garage and showrooms only a few yards away on the opposite side of the road also played an important role with the supply of many smaller sub-assemblies and the larger wing leading edge torsion boxes so essentially a part of the success in the aircraft's design.

Day and night shifts applied to each unit, as it did all the other Spitfire manufacturing sites, with the labour force increasing as the dispersal plan became more fully operative and expanded.

There were changes due to the improved designs made possible by the higher rated Rolls-Royce engines becoming available as well as those dictated as a result of operational flying experiences. These were fed out to the appropriate Areas via the weekly meetings held at the Company's newly dispersed head offices at Hursley Park. To deal with the paperwork distribution involved and any interim documentation or instructions that might arise, an internal postal service was set in motion almost from day one of the moves that distributed and collected from each area every day of the week and used Hursley as its sorting base. Each area had its contacts with its own headquarters and the units within that area.

These arrangements, taking into consideration the troubled times, especially where wide ranging air raids often caused delays to the normal General Post Office system, worked extremely well.

My return to High Post airfield was on March 21st 1943 as the need for the Seafire with catapult facilities was drawing to a conclusion whilst the need for more fighters of the advanced Mark 8 and 9 types were eagerly sought to combat the menace that the FW 190 threatened.

The work was much the same as before so far as the sheetmetal workers were concerned: the cowlings were slightly different, even the fasteners for the cowling panels had an improved design, but overall there was very little that warrants any further clarification.

There is however, one story perhaps worthy of note in case some Spitfire enthusiasts take some of the literature they read too literally, and that only came to light almost fifty years to the day later.

Most of the individual Spitfire histories contained in the book 'Spitfire - The History' are taken from the Air Ministry record cards (known as A.M. Form 78) and according to the card on file for Spitfire serial numbered BR 526 as abbreviated by the authors of this book reads, (without the abbreviation for clarity) 'BR526, production number 3021, built at High Post airfield Salisbury, first flew on the 6th June 1942. Subsequently transferred to 36 Maintenance Unit on the 8th June, and later on the 20th June loaded on to the SS Nigers for transhipment to Takadori where it is re-

Similar to BR526 this is BR375 the 2845th production Spitfire from the Supermarine Group. Built at Salisbury it flew from High Post 22nd April 1942. To Malta 1st August '42 to North Australia 1st June '43 and returned to Middle East in August 1944. Struck off charge 9th May 1945. Was piloted by Len Reid. Photo via H. Wills.

corded as arriving on the 24th July 1942. Then it is shown as SOC (struck off charge) on the 29th August 1942.'

To the historian reading that card it would indicate that either it was damaged beyond repair during shipment (as some were) or that it may have crashed on its early reassembled test flight. Either way SOC spelt that it was gone - and officially forever.

In June 1992 my wife was trawling through our local library for a book suitable for me and she returned with a book entitled 'Against All Odds'; the story of the Australian Air Force's contribution to the Malta defence during its long and bloody siege.

Towards the end of his book, the author, Lex McAuley, goes on to relate how many of the Australians had to be withdrawn to combat the encroaching Japanese menace on their own homeland. McAuley was fortunate to be able to get some of his research from survivors and in some cases from their actual flying log books, and one of the latter regarding a Pilot Officer Tim Goldsmith caught my eye. His squadron, among others was engaged in the air defence of Darwin which the Japanese had been bombing and in the column designated for aircraft type and number was none other than BR 526. His logbook details his engagements with the Japanese aircraft and tells how on March 15th 1943 he shot down two

Jap bombers, and how on the 2nd May whilst flying BR 526 he shot down another before being shot down himself and ending up in the Timor Sea and barely being rescued in time to survive. BR 526 had, of course, found a watery end.

There was something about the aircraft number that caused me to seek out my old works notebooks which I used to record the jobs I did, how long they took, and how much bonus I was due, and there, somewhat to my surprise was the following entry. '8th June 1942, dayshift, BR526, fit top port nose fillet and camera mounting and aperture, with a total of 71/4 hours booked against it.' The next two jobs for the same day were on Seafire MA 974 making a total of 103/4 hours worked for that day.

Now, as the reader will know from what has gone previously, the fillet fitment had to be before the cowling panels could be fitted and cut in to suit, and this would no doubt be done by the following nightshift so on that basis it would have been quite impossible for that aircraft to have been flown until after the Rolls-Royce representative had cleared it and a pilot brought in to test fly it until at the earliest midday on the 9th. This very obviously contradicts the official records, and there is no doubt in my mind as to which record is correct and I insert it purely as a warning that not all official records are correct, or as in this case tells the full story. I attach no blame to the joint authors of Spitfire - The History, they could only use what was available to them and of course neither of them were at Supermarines at any time, but it does parallel for me the omnipotent attitudes adopted by so-called historians as was painfully revealed when Lord Dacre authenticated the Hitler Diary forgeries.

During the period so far reviewed, much similar activities had been taking place in the other areas of dispersal. Eastleigh aerodrome hangars had borne the most of the flight and final assembly for the bulk of the Spitfire production that had successfully seen the R.A.F. through the Battle of Britain and kept pace with the changes due to design modifications or operational refinements. Arthur Nelson presided over the Southampton Area.

The agricultural showroom that the wheeling squad had vacated at the end of May 1941 had been used mainly as a storage space until a new Stores unit had been constructed for them on the Hursley Road and once that had been brought into use the show-room became the site where the first of the Rolls-Royce Griffon engines was fitted to the Spitfire fuselage. This siting was only of a temporary measure as with the main Design Office had by now been located in their own newly built offices in the grounds of Hursley Park, adjacent to the House which was the Company head office, the need for an experimental unit close by became impera-tive and the experimental assembly hangar was built in the Park but closer to the main road. This hangar was supervised by Frank Perry with Bert Diaper as his foreman and staffed by mostly mem-bers of the bombed Southampton works with the wide range of skills that such a leading technology advanced unit would need to function properly. There the new designs were made into reality and the finished products at that time moved on to Worthy Down where the experimental flying team were operating from.

At Newbury a new, purpose built factory was built under Ministry auspices for it to become the major Machine shop facility in the Company and incorporating the very first of the 'Rubber' presses and the relocated 'Ceco' stamping tool, (ex Woolston) as well as its own foundry, the draw bench (also ex Woolston) and numerous machine tools of more recent manufacture to those previously the backbone of the old Woolston machine shop.

This unit became the head office site for Tom Barby who was the Area Manager whilst the unit itself was controlled by Bert Franks as foreman.

Wherever possible changes were made beginning in 1942 to pro-vide the Spitfire production sites with buildings that would enable them either to leave their commandeered garage and bus premises or expand their activities to become as near as possible self con-tained areas. It was never fully achieved as the spread of vital major assemblies or machining dictated by their vulnerability from bombing had to be the overriding factor, nevertheless the network created worked very well and production rose once again back to its original high peak and gradually exceeded it.

By this time the giant 'shadow' factory at Birmingham had at least got rid of its initial problems and come fully on stream as the next chapter relates.

Chapter Five
The 'Shadow Factory

My interest in the Castle Bromwich Spitfire Shadow Factory goes back a long way, as far back as 1938 when I first heard of it, and this interest was greatly stimulated by the editorials of Captain W.E. Johns in the magazine 'Popular Flying' and 'Flying' wherein the very tone of his remarks and criticisms clearly indicated (to me at least) that all was not well. Allow me to quote some examples. From 'Flying' magazine dated 20th August 1938. 'Viscount Nuffield's recent order for 1000 Spitfires has set me thinking. The brain behind the Morris concern may be an excellent one for producing large numbers. But Lord Nuffield has no factory. O.K., he will build one and Sir Kingsley Wood has cut the first turf. That factory must take a year to build, then another six months to get it busy, so no Spitfires for at least 18 months. That's getting on for 1940. The Spitfire came out in 1936!"

December 17th 1938. 'There is a lot of insidious propaganda being introduced into the aircraft works in this country. There is no need to look for the reason. The aircraft factories have become the arteries of the Empire. Should they become poisoned - well we need not dwell on what the results would be. By the grace of Heaven the majority of men in this country are immune against this venom. But there are some who are not. So should these words meet their eyes, let them reflect upon what the assimulation of it may mean, not only to those about them, but to themselves.

On December 31st 1938 under the psuedonym of 'Duty Pilot' for his 'Flying Commentary' article on 'Christmas Gifts' he wrote, 'Father Christmas would make for Kingsway and put a little pep into the Air Ministry's stockings, and a love of flying into the Marshals. He would give Sir Kingsley Wood, the Air Minister, a photograph of himself having his photograph taken, and confer on him the ability to make speeches without looking down at his notes most of the time .....Santa's next objective would be the inner circle of the Society of British Aircraft Constructors, that exclusive body who told the Government that Lord Nuffield was not to build aeroplanes, with the result that the Government had to buy some from America'. John's then goes on about putting German machine tools into the Shadow Factories as British ones are not available, and complains about the shortage of radio-direction finding equipment sets to get RAF machines out of fog and home safely, quoting an example of one lost over its own base last summer. His remarks concluded as follows, 'There would be many other people to be visited - far too many to be mentioned here - and at the end of his tour Father Christmas would have an empty sack. He would find out the officials who are responsible for the deficiencies mentioned above and he would give them all the sack'.

After that blast, which has all the hallmarks of a very frustrated person, Johns editorial of the January 14th 1939 issue, comments, 'It is announced that the Nuffield factory will be in part production in February and full production in August'.

The Flying magazine for the following week had no W.E.J. editorial and the February 25th issue carried a brief note that he was no longer the Editor'.

There is little doubt in my mind now that Captain Johns (ex R.F.C. from the 1914/18 war, and author of the famous 'Biggles' stories) had been sacrificed to placate the Air Minister and the Air Council, and quite possibly the Society of British Aircraft Constructors, at whom he had aimed some telling barbs.

Whether one considers his rather intemperate language and very thinly disguised sarcasm suitable or not, it only became clear long after the war that the basis of his criticism was well founded.

After his removal from the editorial chair the tide of propaganda continued to lull the public into a false sense of security with a series of misleading statements regarding Spitfire production at Castle Bromwich.

We now know that three major aircraft 'Shadow Factories' were built specifically to utilise the motor car industry skills and resources.One at Speke was operated by the Rootes Group and produced Bristol Blenheims, another at Longbridge (Birmingham) and run by the Austin Motor Company built Fairey Battles, and Nuffield's Morris Motor Company at Castle Bromwich to produce Spitfires. The idea of shadowing the production of these types came about once the 1936 re-armament programme was instigated by the Baldwin cabinet. The early discussions were held under the auspices of Sir Phillip Cuncliffe-Lister (later Lord Swinton) the then Air Minister and considerable progress must have resulted as the first Longbridge produced Fairey Battle flew in September 1938 and by the April 22nd 1939 issue of Flying they could report, 'Output .... has proved higher than was originally thought possible. Less than 20 were expected by the end of 1938, but the total reached 50. Production has now reached its peak'.

In respect of the Speke effort the May 1939 issue has a photo of a very full organised finals production line. 'Flight' the aviation journal for December 14th 1939 shows an even better picture with the comment 'From grassland to production in twelve months'. added in a post-war reprint.

Of the Castle Bromwich factory, this was the comment from Flying in an article on the Spitfire dated 20th May 1939. 'Today these aircraft are passing into use and into reserve in formidable numbers - not to be hinted at. The only light... is a statement by Sir Kingsley Wood when he cut the first sod of Lord Nuffield's shadow factory at Castle Bromwich July 15th 1938. Sir K.W. then revealed the 1000 order'. The articles author, Wiliam Courtenay added, 'Before the end of this year we shall see the first of these on parade'. This was followed on June 15th 1939 by the caption under a photograph of Lord Nuffield stating, 'whose aircraft factory will shortly begin production of high speed fighters'.

If we add to these comments those current at the time from no less than Winston Churchill about the parlous position of our air defences, and in particular its Fighter Defence Forces, it becomes fairly clear that something was amiss - and badly so.

In retrospect, and with the blessed advantage of hindsight, it is mainly the failure of the giant Castle Bromwich factory to produce the very soon to be vital Spitfires that was mainly exercising the minds of politicians, Ministries, and very senior R.A.F. officers once war was declared.

My perplexity begins with the fact that it was common public knowledge early in 1938, as evidenced by the excerpts I have quoted, that an order for 1000 Spitfires had been made on the Nuffield organised Castle Bromwich shadow factory and yet the official Contract document for this very large order was not signed until April 12th 1939 under its number B981687/39. Was it that the situation was so silly that Kingsley Wood cut the first sod for the factory in the previous July in the full knowledge that it would take a full year to build and equip such a project, leaving Nuffield with nothing in the way of financial and contract cover to commence simultaneously the provisioning of tools, materials etc. until the factory was built, or had there been an ITP (intention to proceed) notice issued to enable this kind of preparatory work to commence? Nowhere in any of the enquiries I have made has this been revealed. Neither has there been any official confirmation that the first ten 'delivered'? from Castle Bromwich were in fact ten taken from the Supermarine production line at Eastleigh which was revealed in my book in 1985, and as we shall see subsequently substantiated in greater detail in Mr. Scruby's letter of 1987; and since in another letter to me which states, 'I heard all about the 10 in June episode from Wilf Elliott and got the impression that he regarded the presentation of the engraved lighters as a priceless joke, but also that anything produced from that place was a worthy of a memorial! It was, of course, regarded by him as about the funniest thing of all time that he should receive an engraved lighter for turning out in June ten aircraft which had been largely produced in his own works'.

Why Alex Henshaw, the test pilot seconded from Supermarines to take over the test flying at Castle Bromwich, does not mention this in his book, and even the 'definitive' Spitfire - The History fails to account for the 'switching' is past my comprehension.

If we take the 'official' facts as true; the first sod cut for the factory in July 1938 and the contract placement in April 1939 it must mean that the factory took about ten months to build, which is pretty good going, and then only fifteen months to produce tooling, make details, assemble and flight test their own first Spitfires, with mainly personnel at all levels who had no experience of aircraft production before. That would have been extremely good if it were true, but here my doubts creep in based on my own knowledge and experience in similar situations of production management on other aircraft.

If we accept that the Supermarine contract for 310 Spitfires was signed on the 3rd June 1936 (which in effect was little more than an Instruction to Proceed as the detailed Specification for the aircraft was not received by the Company until July 28th 1936, and contained 33 changes including such important items as increasing the leading edge wing skin thickness, fuel tank capacity to be increased, and wing tips and fuselage end bay to be detachable) the first flight of No.1 Production Spitfire took place at Eastleigh on 14th May 1938 i.e. twenty three months. We know that this aircraft, as did many of its successors, suffered from the bugbears of constant modifications - all no doubt reasonably justified in the circumstances prevailing at the time - as the prototype continued to undergo various Air Ministry tests at Martlesham in parallel with the production build.

Nuffield's production management tackled their order very similarly to their car production methods, by tooling up to a far greater degree than Supermarines with greater usage of big press tools and even smaller press tooling to compensate for the shortage they must have experienced of the requisite skilled labour. These tools take time to design and make and in many instances defeat their main object as soon as some modification is called for.

I feel certain that when the order was placed for the build of the factory, and the announcement made of the 1000 aircraft order, that some contractual arrangement was given, even though it only be in the form of a letter of intent, that authorised Nuffield to go ahead and start procuring the tooling and materials from the drawings that would have been available from Supermarines by then. Sir Kingsley Wood is said to have spoken to Lord Nuffield and agreed this scheme, but when the shadow scheme was first mooted he did not hold the Air Minister's position and there is ample evidence that most of the early discussions took place with Lord Swinton who certainly instigated the Longbridge and Speke shadow factories with their respective owners.

Was the Nuffield factory delayed for some reason. We now know that there was an awful lot of dithering at the Air Council level as to whether the Supermarine production should be maintained or curtailed and this was what W.E. Johns was so furious about and which for speaking out so plainly he was removed from his editorial post. I am informed that it was something similar that eventually removed both Sir Robert McLean and Trevor Westbrook from their positions, although they did it less publicly.

This 'fiddling whilst Rome burned' is apparent from a letter to the Air Ministry as late as March 1939 from Alan Clifton, Mitchell's Head of Technical Development and by this time second in command at Supermarines to Joe Smith, the Chief Designer. He wrote, 'I attach a specification of an improved Spitfire..... This has been prepared in the hope that it may assist us to obtain further production orders for Supermarine to follow the present contracts, a matter about which I am most concerned.' It continues later. 'Our own orders total 710 which will be delivered about a year from now, and Nuffield will then be starting regular deliveries of his contract for 1000 off'. But this is a month before the Nuffield Contract date.

Then there is the report in the January 14th 1939 of 'Flying' as mentioned previously that 'It is announced that the Nuffield factory will be in part production in February and in full production in August'. Who made that announcement? And how could they say such a thing when the Contract was not signed until the following April?

Frankly I am of the opinion that the Castle Bromwich factory for building Spitfires was arranged under the auspices as Longbridge and Speke and at the same time, long before Sir Kingsley Wood came onto the scene. It is most likely that Nuffield and his people wanted to be free of the normal complications of the aircraft industry and desired to do their 1000 order in their own way, and in pursuing that course ran into difficulties that required experienced Spitfire personnel to assist them.

Stanley Woodley was sent there by Elliott as a Liaison Officer, as he stated in his contribution to the Royal Aeronautical Society's Symposium to celebrate the Spitfire's 40th anniversary in 1976, and at least two others known to me went there from 'K' shop at Woolston.

Three fuselages were sent to Birmingham as pattern guides for the workers to physically see how things went together. Woodley says that he arranged swops of parts between the Woolston and Castle Bromwich works and I can recall using and seeing some of the CB parts at Woolston. This indicates to me that the detail manufacturing and some of the smaller sub-assemblies were being produced in plentiful numbers, but that the main component build was not up to programme.

Trying to pin down why the main component production lines were delayed has proved most difficult. We knew at Woolston from the information that was being fed back from our ex-colleagues now working at CB that there were a lot of squabbles over money - in particular bonus payments. Being used to the car industry's piecework pricing, or alternatively the straight bonus scheme that operated on the basis of 'what you saved was all the operators to keep' as opposed to the scheme we at Southampton worked to where there was a 'safety' contingency built into the time allowed from the start and 'what was saved under this scheme was shared in equal portions with the management, or employer', the Birmingham workers wanted 'our' times but not the final split with the employer. Somewhere along the line, no doubt in an effort to get some peace and quiet and some tangible production, their frustrated management gave in, thus allowing the workers to earn very much more than Supermarine's workers were getting, or alternatively taking much longer to do the same jobs without being financially worse off.

In a series of articles in one of the main Birmingham newspapers in 1964, Mr. Bonar Dickson recalled, 'When pay became a problem in 1942, not too little, but too much! Apparently the sheet metal workers were picking up £25 per week. Even the Coventry workers were embarrassed, and piecework rates were limited, with the Shop Stewards agreement, to average £17 per week. At Castle Bromwich an hourly rate of 5/- was established'. (Mr. Dickson was the man put in to run the Castle Bromwich factory when Vickers were given instructions from Beaverbrook to manage it in May 1940).

Compare the above with the 1/10d per hour Southampton and Eastleigh were earning - in present day coinage the equivalent of 25p against 9p. Even with this largesse the Birmingham employees went on strike in 1942 and had to be spoken to rather sharply by a senior Union man at the request of Sir Stafford Cripps, the then Minister of Aircraft Production.

It is little wonder that no one seems to want to answer pertinent questions on this subject for the period leading up to the critical Battle of Britain.

When Churchill took over the Premiership in May 1940 one of his first tasks was to divorce the aircraft production responsibilities from the Air Ministry. This he did by creating the new Ministry of Aircraft Production and placing it in the hands of Lord Beaverbrook and virtually giving him a free rein to cut through the tangled web of bureaucratic red tape and clear up the 'aircraft scandal' to use Churchill's own words.

Beaverbrook was a very controversial and peculiar choice for this position. His reputation was none too inspiring according to his biographers, as it appears that he left his Canadian homeland with the strong smell of a major financial scandal behind him and integrated himself into British life mainly through his Daily Express newspaper. He had no experience of the aircraft industry, but what he could do, and did, was select men who had.

Almost his first task was to have Sir Richard Fairey go to Castle Bromwich and report back to him personally the situation there - Sir Richard having successfully created and operated a 'shadow' aircraft factory on the opposite side of Birmingham to construct Fairy Battle bombers. That report confirmed what both Churchill and Beaverbrook feared and galvanised the new minister into action.

Three days after his appointment Beaverbrook rang Lord Nuffield demanding to know why no Spitfires had emerged from the Castle Bromwich factory. The best account of what transpired between the two men is stated in Alfred Price's book, 'The Spitfire Story' where the author relates the conversation as heard by Sir Miles Thomas (then Nuffield's Vice Chairman) who just happened to be with Nuffield when he took Beaverbrook's call. In essence the conversation got acrimonious and Nuffield foolishly said sarcastically 'Perhaps you would like me to give up the Spitfire factory?' and the 'Beaver' nipped in smartly and replied 'Thank you very much, I accept' and slammed the phone down. Vickers were then charged with the management of the whole of the Birmingham Spitfire production.

Even Vickers did not get an easier ride from Beaverbrook and they found it necessary to send ten completed Spitfires to Castle Bromwich so that they could meet, or appease, the constant telephone demands for results, often in the middle of the night to the very senior executives. It was nothing less than bully-boy tactics, but in view of the critical situation that was facing the country at the time probably the only way to achieve results in that particular field and so justifiable.

Which brings us to the famous or infamous '10 in June' story. "Spitfire - The History' has no record of this piece of artful trickery, mainly because their information is gathered from the 'official' Ministry returns, and as one can imagine no one at that time was likely to report the facts in case Beaverbrook got hold of it. The Ministry Form 70 returns apparently show only 6 Spitfires delivered from Castle Bromwich for June 1940 although 10 had been signalled.

The procedure was then, that after the company's test pilot had flown and cleared an aircraft (this might include more than one flight) the on site A.I.D. inspector would make his final checks and issue a form taking the aircraft onto the Ministry's charge, thus permitting the firm to signal its completion and usually request a pilot to remove it to an RAF Maintenance Storage Unit.

There appears to be some confusion in 'Spitfire - The History' as it shows only six Spitfires leaving Castle Bromwich bearing a June delivery date and it only credits nine Spitfires all told as 'Morris' built, P7280 to P7288, notwithstanding their recording the first Vickers managed delivery as P7289 on the 17th July 1940, but also showing three others P7300, P7301 and P7302 being delivered during the first three days in July, i.e. two weeks prior to the first Vickers aircraft.

Whatever occurred, there is little doubt that the management changes were justified as indeed was the separation of the aircraft production responsibilities from the bureaucratically moribund Air Ministry. Beaverbrook distanced himself from the Whitehall constrictions by establishing his Ministry in his own London residence, Stornaway House and gathered round him a team of his own choosing. This team included, Sir Charles Craven, the former Managing Director of Vickers Armstrong and Air Marshall Sir Wilfred Freeman, previously the joint heads of the Department of Development and Production from the Air Ministry; three civil servants whom he considered best to bring order out of the administrative chaos, Mr. Edmund Compton, Eaton Griffiths and Sir Archibald Rowlands. Around this core he added two personal secretaries, George Thomson from the Express newspaper and David Farrar, Beaverbrook's political secretary, his news editor J.B. Wilson from the Express and Lord Brownlow as his Parliamentary Private Secretary. The aircraft 'professional muscle' came from industry's Trevor Westbrook; and the man who probably had the best knowledge of production lines and factory management at that time, Patrick Hennessy of Fords. Many others were recruited to be 'overseers' at most of the aircraft factories responsible for reporting back each day to Beaverbrook the situation existing wherever they were located and when Beaverbrook thought necessary to cajole or bully the managements into greater effort. This latter facet caused a certain amount of friction with some of the in-situ managements who were quite capable of handling their own affairs and the fact that some of these 'overseers' abused their powers - in one case at Supermarines by demanding they kept him liberally supplied with his favourite alcoholic beverage.

However, in the matter of Castle Bromwich there can be little room for doubt that Beaverbrook's intervention was vitally necessary to lance the festering self inflicted wounds, and with this he had the weighty support from Churchill himself as evidenced by the appendices in Churchill's 'The Second World War, Volume Two.'

Whatever occurred, and however it was achieved there, matters little when compared to the results, nevertheless, even today little has come to light regarding the steps that must have been taken to break the bottlenecks that had been orchestrated by politically motivated persons to delay the output of the aircraft that were so vital in a manner that bordered on treason.

From the moment that the Vickers management took charge a gradual trickle of Spitfires in that fateful June soon became a flood; albeit after the Battle of Britain, but was fortunately timed to take up the period after the Woolston and Itchen works were bombed and the delays incurred during the subsequent dispersals when their production sagged from 340 for the quarter year up to the end of September 1940 to 170 in the following quarter. Even that reduction was fortuitous as the Germans had failed miserably in their attempts to bomb the Spitfire assembly hangars at Eastleigh aerodrome where the old, American built, first World War hangars bore a charmed life and remained untouched throughout the whole of the war.

By the time the Battle of Britain was to all intents and purposes over, say by the end of October 1940, the Castle Bromwich factory from which so much had been expected had delivered only 195 Spitfires and of these only a few dozen participated in the latter end of that critical struggle. The fact that by February 1941 they had delivered over 600 odd was, by then, neither here nor there, but that very total gives a good indication to just how many part finished aircraft must have been held up in the production pipeline for one reason or another. It is a sorry tale that leaves a nasty taste in the mouth even after all the years between, and is worth remembering when one watches on television the 1976 programme made to extol the 'gloriest' efforts of that particular Works.

Apart from the foregoing, Beaverbrook and his team did build on an original idea of Lord Nuffield's to have the Aircraft Repair Organisation under civilian control, which was a great success, and they were also instrumental in having women from all over the country drafted into the aircraft factories. Beaverbrook was also responsible for the appeal to housewives to hand over their aluminium pots and pans saying "We will turn your pots and pans into Spitfires and Hurricanes" and although the housewives responded magnificently the campaign was hardly necessary since there was plenty of scrap aluminium available and the poor housewives' sacrifices negligible and their material unsuited to aircraft requirements.

The Beaverbrook Spitfire Appeal - buy a Spitfire for £5000 - soon brought in £1,000,000 per month, but the contributors never quite realised that their money could not put Spitfires into the skies.

Beaverbrook was however an inveterate myth builder, none more so to his own glorification. He reported to the War Cabinet that at the time of his appointment as Minister of Aircraft Production there had only been "45 aircraft ready for service and now there are 1040." This is absolute rubbish and he must have known it. Hawkers had been building Hurricanes in greater numbers, and longer, than the Spitfires of Supermarines, and even allowing for the Hurricane casualties that arose during the battles in France - to which Lord Dowding wisely refused to permit Spitfires to be sent - there must have been available in May 1940 somewhere in the region of 1000 Hurricanes and 700 Spitfires overall even if one third of these were allocated to Service Squadrons and two thirds in Reserve this gives a substantially different picture than Beaverbrook was painting. The post-war information reveals quite clearly that the increase in aircraft production was gathering pace even before his Lordship came on the scene.

In 1974 the R.A.F. official history shows the following:-

	Production of all types	Production of Fighters
Feb 1940	719	141
March	860	177
April	1081	256
May	1279	325
June	1591	446
July	1665	496
August	1601	476

The figures speak for themselves and confirm, if confirmation was necessary, that the increased production credit belongs to those men and managements who had laid its foundations years before.

In their biography 'Beaverbrook', the authors Anne Chisholm and

The large Castle Bromwich factory Spitfire building shop. Vickers.

Michael Davies (Pub. Hutchinson 1992) state: 'Beaverbrook ran the Ministry of Aircraft Production for eleven months. His successor, Moore-Brabazon, although a Beaverbrook admirer, later wrote; "When I arrived at the MAP, for some reason things were not going too well. The Air Ministry and MAP were scarcely on speaking terms, so to speak, and as our sole reason for existing was to supply the R.A.F. with planes, this struck me as rather ridiculous."

From all the foregoing it is obvious that no one person can be blamed for ills that beset Castle Bromwich for it was a sickness that was spread over Ministries, Managements, Unions that were politically motivated, where their combined miasma detracted from the efforts of the majority of the workforce who intended well, and deprived the nation of much needed Spitfires at the most critical time.

Once the transfer of authority was passed to Vickers they moved in with commendable speed, appointing at first some of their directors to oversee the initial changes that were warranted such as making Mr. Talamo and Wilfred Elliot as Joint General Managers (the latter still officially Works Manager at Southampton), retain-

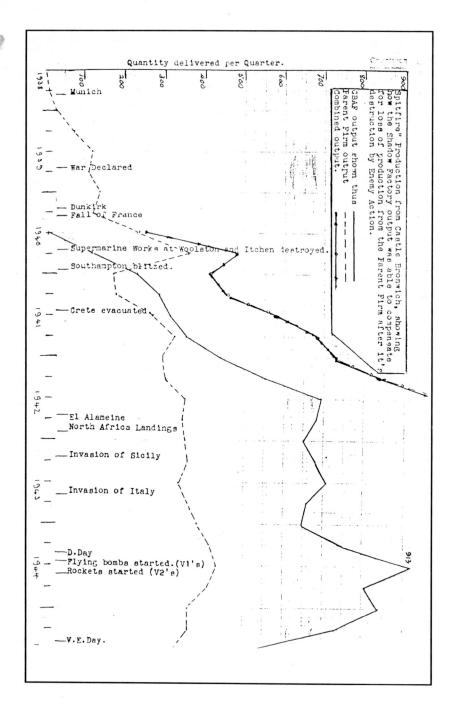

Quantity delivered per Quarter.

"Spitfire" Production from Castle Bromwich, showing
how the Shadow Factory output was able to compensate
for loss of production from the Parent Firm after it's
destruction by Enemy Action.

CBAF output shown thus
Parent Firm output
Combined output.

1938 — Munich

1939 — War Declared

— Dunkirk
— Fall of France

1940 — Supermarine Works at Woolston and Itchen destroyed.

— Southampton blitzed.

1941 — Crete evacuated

1942 — El Alameine
— North Africa Landings

— Invasion of Sicily

1943 — Invasion of Italy

— D.Day
1944 — Flying bombs started.(V1's)
— Rockets started (V2's)

— V.E.Day.

ing Bernard Cook as Works Manager for the Castle Bromwich factory and transferring Alex Henshaw as its Chief Test pilot. Wilfred Elliot spent a considerable amount of his working time at the Castle Bromwich factory, introducing into its organisation men from the Southampton area to stay on a permanent basis to provide the lead required by the circumstances existing at the time and yet there has never been any acknowledgement, so far as I can trace, of his efforts to bring about the massive improvement that was necessary, and indeed was achieved. He still kept himself in touch with the situation at Southampton by telephone and telex with his Assistant there, and this situation remained until the onset of the actual air raids that indicated that the Southampton factories were clearly a Luftwaffe target. Vickers eventually appointed B.W.A. Dickson as the Castle Bromwich General Manager who remained there until the end of the war, and as mentioned previously was largely responsible for bringing a reduction in the excessive pay demands that had prevailed.

I referred earlier to a Mr Scruby's letter, and I have left its inclusion until now as it covers both the site where the prototype Spitfire was built - always something of a mystery for years - and confirms independently the matter of the '10 in June'. This is how it was transmitted to me, and as it has that ring of truth I will quote it verbatim.

"Perhaps the following may assist as I was fortunate to be on the prototype Spitfire from start to finish and ultimately helped to equip all the Squadrons on maintenance procedures and repairs.

The first fuselage was built in 'K' shop adjacent to Fanny Penton's Dope shop, and surrounded by green tarpaulins. Needless to say everybody found a good excuse for coming to have a look. Four of us made the first fuselage after the main jig had been built by the toolroom, Ken Scales, George Guard, another plus myself.

The wings were built in the Wing shop and fitted together with the Merlin engine in 'K' shop. For security reasons the engine was tested at night by Gibson of Rolls-Royce after we had secured the tailskid to one of the rings on the patio used for parking Southampton and Scapa flying boats.

The noise and flames from the then, stub exhausts, were terrific. We dismantled the wings and wooden propeller and then reassembled the plane in the workshop at Eastleigh, where incidentally, the S6b was stored less engine.

When completed the A.I.D. would not pass the functioning of the wheel locks in the wings with the Oleo legs retracted, so we got authority to let Mutt Summers make a taxying test with the wheels lashed together with a tourniquet of rope, i.e. locked down. The taxying was OK and without authority Mutt came racing towards the hangar and took off at full boost, screaming over our heads to the delight of R.J.M. and T.C.L.W.

Ken Scales went to Martlesham Heath during the trials, and when K 5054 was being flown by W/C J.F. McKenna, he had a dead seize of the Merlin engine and managed to put it down with the wheels up on the Heath. The plane was brought back by Supermarine transport and all the photographs are in the Spitfire museum at Southampton.

After the repairs I was at Martlesham for nearly a year and Ken Scales was put in charge of production at Eastleigh.

He then went to Castle Bromwich and I was asked to go as Dixon's (Dickson. Author) assistant. This I refused, having been made Chief Service Engineer for Spitfires and Wellington Squadrons based on Vickers House.

The first ten Spitfires from CBAF were actually made at Southampton, dismantled and reassembled at CBAF. Ken Scales was given a suitably inscribed watch to commemorate this great feat!"

The recipient of this interesting letter which he has so kindly passed its content to me continues that " 'Young' Scruby did well and later joined Beaverbrook's team as Personal Assistant to Trevor Westbrook and Technical Assistant to Sir John Buchanan who was Director General under Sir Charles Craven."

Apparently Mr Scruby's letter was written in 1987, when he was 74 years old and having long retired from the prominent positions that he had previously held in industry, many of which I understand to have been associated with the career of Trevor Westbrook. Whilst Ken Scales was away at Castle Bromwich the onus of responsibility for the foremanship at the Eastleigh flight shed fell on Nigel Johnson who continued in that position for the remainder of the war after Scales was appointed Area Manager at Reading.

The final part to the Castle Bromwich jigsaw which has come to my attention was a letter from Mr. F. Shelley which appeared as recently as the Autumn issue of the Spitfire Society's Journal.

I wrote to Mr. Shelley and he has very kindly sent me a copy of his book 'A Grain of Sand' from which I am quoting for the relevant part.

"I had finished all my apprenticeship involvements at Austin Motor Company and was offered several good appointments within the firm but I felt I wanted to gain extra experiences. My father arranged interviews for me and I could have settled on any of a selection of posts.

At about this time, March 1938, news was being displayed of an aircraft factory being developed at Dunlop Works, Tyburn. I attended the interview and was immediately offered a job to start the following Monday. At my start I found I was the third employee to be engaged, there was a manager, Mr. Day and one other draughtsman. I was immediately handed the project of planning and designing equipment to produce the Spitfire engine mounting. Every week more and more staff joined the Company. We were working in an old wooden shed belonging to Dunlop but was the start of Castle Bromwich Aeroplane Co. Ltd., to production build Spitfires. By now I had eight draughtsmen working for me and I was appointed section leader. We had rough sketches and plans of Abe Mitchell and early drawings of the plane Abe specified the schedules of the wings and the joining of the projection lines .... We were also given details of the engine size and measurements and told that the equipment would have to accept the possibility of increase in power of the Merlin Engines............. The section continued to design a checking fixture to include all the salient location points. The jig when complete was ordered and production pressure produced an estimate in those days of £20,000.

- 131 -

Before the jig was delivered production requirements ordered twelve to be available, one to remain as a master check fixture only. We were all anxious and deeply conscious of the consequences of any mistake. The first fixture was delivered and Southampton sent up a sample engine mounting that was reported to be perfect and if it fitted into the fixture all would be well. The position of the mounting was established and all gate position and plungers slapped home one at a time. Only one seemed in error, the engine mounting was then set up and a very small fault found in the original pattern. When corrected the jig was absolutely perfect to all our relief."

Fred Shelley went on to work for B.S.A. on gun barrels and subsequently rose to Assistant Superintendent at B.S.A., then Toolroom Manager of the Bristol Aeroplane Company's Rodney Works, and finally Chairman and Managing Director of the Kings Heath Engineering Group of companies in Birmingham.

His account seemed to indicate quite clearly that some form of contract cover existed with the Nuffield people as early as March 1938 that set the tooling up process in motion ages before the 'official' contract was issued, and if current accounts prevailing at the time are to be believed, before even the Castle Bromwich factory site building's first sod was cut.

Chapter Six - A Management View

My manuscript had been mostly completed by the time Denis Webb so generously presented me with four chapters from his own and as they are written in his own inimitable style, and from a different viewpoint than my own I decided to incorporate them at the most convenient place within mine and in his own words wherever I could. Having in the foregoing given my interpretation up to the end of 1943, or nearly, I present his next contribution which he has chapter headed as:-

The Dispersal

The first day in the Polygon got things moving. Pratt was still out of action. Being blown from one side of the railway embankment to the other at Itchen at over fifty years of age had not done him much good and he had injured his hand fairly badly.

However, Wilfred Elliot, Wing Commander Kellett, the Air Ministry Overseer, with Whitehead and Cowley (Beaverbrook's men) got together and decided on the next move which was to send senior staff men (who were not actively engaged in getting things settled in the Southampton area, such as Winchester Road out in various directions to hunt for suitable buildings within sixty miles, to house Wing jigs, Fuselage jigs and Machine tools, as well as some suitable for fuselage assembly and final erection. They were to take note of dimensions and type of construction as well as facilities such as electricity and water, sanitation and ease of access, and to report back as quickly as possible.

As the information came in it was collated and recorded by Len Gooch, the Works Engineer who had his record of plant and equipment so he could roughly check which buildings would prove most suitable. The allocation of buildings for wing jigs was, of course, dictated by clear internal height.

Immediately it had been decided which buildings we wanted the owners were phoned and our intention to requisition made known - if any obstruction occurred, the 'big guns' were brought to bear in the shape of either Cowley or Whitehead. Even after requisitioning some owners played awkward but their efforts were ineffectual.

With the choice of sites and area settled, various foremen were chosen to act as Area Managers. Those so chosen were Bill Heaver for Salisbury, Hall for Trowbridge, Scales for Reading and Tom Barby for Newbury and Hungerford. Winchester was treated as being part of the Southampton Area under Nelson.

Requisitioning some places proved difficult as they had already been requisitioned by other Government Departments who were very loathe to part with them. One such place in Winchester had already been requisitioned by the Ministry of Food, and Len Gooch made me laugh with his description of Cowley's conversation over the phone with the Food Ministry man. "What have yer got stored there?" went the slow Canadian drawl. Silence, then "Pineapples?!" with a rising inflection of exasperation. "Jesus! Do you think you can win this goddam war with PINEAPPLES!"

We got the premises the next day, but in some cases I believe Churchill had to be brought into the business.

Cowley would cheerfully have requisitioned any buildings we wanted or even one we didn't want! One day looking out of the Polygon Hotel he cast a covetous eye on the Guildhall! "Gee, that would make a swell erecting shop" he said! Wilf Elliot persuaded him to leave it alone.

Another difficult place to acquire was the Wilts and Dorset bus garage in Salisbury, which with its clear height was ideal for Spitfire wing jigs. In this case the Mayor of Salisbury was supposed to have objected strongly, so Cowley made some preliminary investigations and then rang the Mayor.

Again Len Gooch came into the office laughing at the conversation he had just listened to and imitated it for my benefit.

"Tell me Mr. Mayor" said Cowley. "I believe you are the Patron of the local Spitfire Fund - Is that true?" "Oh yes" came the obviously proud reply. "Well," said Cowley, with his inimitable drawl, "May I suggest that you close that fund and start another to erect a statue to the Mayor who thought Spitfires weren't necessary!"

and quietly put the receiver down! Capitulation followed soon afterwards.

Cowley was a great character - always calm and unruffled and with a great sense of humour. I think we all liked him immensely. Whitehead was a different kettle of fish and I don't think anyone cared for him much. I certainly didn't! For one thing he was far too keen on whiskey at the firm's expense! The Hotel kept on putting chits into our office for signature which was to cover bottles of whiskey ordered by Whitehead - at our expense! Most of Elliot's paperwork landed on my desk and so in due course they came to me for signature. One day I scrawled across the chit 'Not Supermarines - try Mr Whitehead' and initialled it. Whitehead was most displeased and complained to Elliot who in turn said "You shouldn't have done that," so I said "Why not - why in hell's name should we pay for his bloody whiskey - doesn't Beaverbrook pay him enough?" "Oh well!" said Elliot. "It helps keep the peace." Anyway no more chits came to me for signature but the atmosphere between us became rather cool. I am afraid there was a mutual antipathy between us. Not having seen him for several days I bumped into him one Saturday afternoon as I was leaving the hotel to go home for a change. "Where are you off to?" says Whitehead. "Home" says I. "Surprised you have the time" says he. "Haven't seen you lately" says I. "Had a cold" says he. "Lucky you" says I, "I haven't had time to catch a cold!" and went on my way. Fortunately we didn't see much of him.

While we were at the Polygon we nearly got clouted again on the 5th November when a lone raider came over and dropped a bomb which struck the corner of the Civic Centre just across the park from the hotel.

Arthur Nelson and I were in our office when we heard the whistle start and dived for the stairs. We must have reached nearly 'terminal velocity' as we descended the stairs to the ground floor as we got there at almost the same time as the 'Woomph'.

We soon learnt that the bomb had hit the Art School and killed a number of children. Shortly afterwards, as I went along Winchester Road, a labourer from the Wing shop said "Is it true that the Civic Centre has been hit Mr. Webb?" I confirmed this and added

I understood it had hit the Art School, at which information he looked as though he would pass out any moment. "Christ! my kid's there today" he said. So I told him to tell his foreman what I had told him "and go there yourself to see if she is all right." About two days later when I next saw him he confirmed what we had both feared - his kid had been killed.

Much of my time began to be taken up with problems of petrol rationing. All employees who had to use their cars to get to work had to have their Log Books marked and to get forms signed by the firm to show the application was genuine. Many of these came to Elliot as Works Manager and of course landed up on my desk. With people being moved to different places of work there were endless requests for extra rations and I was being stopped on my way round Southampton with cries for help! Somehow I managed to keep the peace with them all, which may have been the reason for a new job several months later.

The description of our early dispersal and subsequent recovery after the bombing, which appears in Andrew & Morgan's book on page 336 is about as far from the truth as it could possibly be! This is no reflection on the integrity of the authors who can only use the materials they are given.

I am pretty sure where the information came from because it bears a remarkable resemblance to the tales which Len Gooch recounted to me years after the war when we met at a retirement party. On that occasion he rolled his eyes in a peculiar way and went into what appeared to be a trance and then described the heroic deeds done in dispersing the factory, quite oblivious of the fact that I had been working in the same office as he had at the Polygon Hotel, and that at first he had passed proposed layouts over to me for my views until I told him to stop wasting time but to give the rough layout to the foreman who would be running the shop and let them make the final decisions on the spot.

His descriptions of what happened and how quickly he had got things back to normal bore no resemblance to reality, but he seemed happy with this fantasy and so I saw no point in bringing him down to earth! Strangely, I found recently on reading a book by C.R. Russell about his life at Supermarines, that he had had ex-

actly the same sort of experience and I quote from his book "............
although he recognised me he did not seem to know where from
and he rambled on about his achievements at Southampton, talking with his eyes fixed about a foot over my head, looking into
space, a mannerism he adopted when expounding about himself
and giving me in effect, exactly the same contribution that he made
later on the 40th Anniversary of the Spitfire prototype's first flight
Symposium held at the Southampton University in 1976, barely
three months before his death ...."

The danger in this is that historians may latch on to his fantasising and then we shall, unfortunately, have to agree with Henry
Ford's dictum that 'History is Bunk.'

I agree with everything C.R. Russell says on this matter. Len
Gooch's fantasising has already been accepted as history and put
into print as such and so in fairness to those whose initiative and
hard work got things going, I will try and record the real facts - not
just from memory, but with the aid of notes prepared for Wilfred
Elliot, the Works Manager at the time and my boss at the time.

Before I start I would like to emphasise that Len Gooch worked
extremely hard and accomplished much and whatever his faults
his heart was in the right place in as much as his main interest
was in the success of the Firm and its products. The bombing and
his work with Beaverbrook's representatives provided just the opportunity which he rightly seized, but this opportunity put him
into a position which he would never normally have held as he
had no experience of aircraft production! His job had been to
design special machinery and look after plant and equipment and
such like and so he had nothing to do with aircraft production at
all. If he had been in charge of the Jig and Tool Drawing Office or
had been the Chief Planner it would have been a different matter.
The manner of his promotion is dealt with in the next chapter.

Now, let us review some of the statements in Andrew and Morgan's
book which is otherwise a marvellous reference book. The book
says, "Len Gooch had planned a complete production line in Southampton premises and it was put into operation by Gilbert Olsen, a
young foreman, whose organising ability played a vital role in the
complex operation of building an advanced fighter in a well dis-

persed series of unlikely workshops by people who were not necessarily skilled aircraft workers. This dispersal was virtually completed by 20th September 1940."

This is utter rubbish - there was no proper dispersal before the raid on the 24th September. As already mentioned, dispersal was completely against the Firm's policy until Castle Bromwich were really and truly going strong.

What we had done was to earmark several buildings such as Hendy's Garage in Poundtree Road, Seward's Garage in Winchester Road and another garage in Shirley. We had done some preliminary work on black out and such like and even put some spare jigs in place, but to call it a production line is preposterous. There was no wing production to start with - it wasn't until we got all the Fire Brigade Trailer Pumps moved out of the Hants and Dorset bus garage in Winchester Road after I had had a row with the Deputy Town Clerk and we had also moved some 400 tons of sandbags out that we began to move wing jigs into the place. We did not move into the Sunlight Laundry until after the raids and Carey and Lamberts also was not a working proposition by the 20th or even the 24th.

The Quarterly Report to the Board for December 1940 confirms my recollections, as it states:-

Dispersal of Production

"On instructions given us by the Minister of Aircraft Production dispersal was proceeded with immediately after the damage by enemy action on the Woolston and Itchen Works on September 26th.

Three premises in Southampton having already been requisitioned and partly prepared, dispersal to these three premises took place immediately which enabled a certain amount of production to continue. By the end of October dispersal was completed to a total of twenty-two workshops and seven premises used as Stores". The underlining is mine.

The resumption of work on the fuselage construction was a quick affair as they were very easy to move and re-site and reference and all the men had to do was to go on doing what they had done before. The main problem here was getting sufficient supplies of compressed air for the riveters and this was overcome, until proper compressors could be obtained, by requisitioning compressors as used by road, and other contractors, and in some cases linking them together and running long lengths of hoses into the workshops while the compressors roared away outside to the discomfort of the residents!

We also had some difficulty in getting enough coupons for the fuel until various officials were beaten over the head!

Resumption of work on fuselage installation and equipping was also fairly straightforward as all we had to do was to transport the fuselages and their trestles to the new premises together with the men and their benches who then carried on doing what they normally did. Here we had a certain amount of trouble because to save possible loss after part of the Finished Part Store at Itchen had been damaged in the raid on the 26th I had told the storekeepers to get all the parts out of the store and taken to huts we had taken over in Hollybrook Road and dump it so the fitters could find the parts they normally fitted and carry on while we sorted it all back into storage bins later.

The 'unlikely workshops' in the Southampton area were mostly very suitable having been garage workshops, and the 'worker not necessarily skilled in aircraft work' were, in fact, our own employees, although later, of course we had to recruit more people.

The whole story is unfair to the memory of people like Arthur Nelson, Bill Heaver, Vernon Hall, George Gingell, Frank Barnett, Tom Barby, Ken Scales, Syd Bloxham, Bill Peckham to mention only a few, as well as men like Jock Stewart and his maintenance gang. It was their years of experience and ability to improvise and all round engineering know-how which enabled premises and equipment to be adapted to our needs, and I have no doubt that many feats of ingenuity were performed by the men on the shop floor.

The legend which seems to have built up about the splendid forward planning which made the dispersal such a success also needs correcting. This in no way lessens the good work done by Gooch, but quite apart from the fact the legend makes no mention of Wilfred Elliot, under whose wise guidance Len Gooch worked, it overlooks the simple fact that until the scouts had come back from their search for suitable premises (after the bombing) and the places had been chosen, did anyone have any idea of which town we were going into, much less which building! How then could any pre-planning take place?

As one who worked with Wilf Elliot for many years and was with him at the Polygon, I can say quite definitely that it was not pre-planning which made the dispersal successful, but the quite marvellous improvisation and hard work that did the trick. In a way it was like Dunkirk - a disaster overcome by improvisation and guts!

In this respect I might add that at Supermarines, the several years during which we built aircraft while having the factory rebuilt around us had made us all rather good at improvisation! The moving of plant and equipment into the requisitioned premises was one of the easier jobs. More difficult was the moving of people. Temporary lodgings had to be found for hundreds of men in each area. Obviously married men transferred to a safe area would not work well, or at all, if their wives and children were still in Southampton. So apart from requisitioning houses, prefabricated houses were put up in the various areas.

The Quarterly Report to the Board for March 4th 1941 records that:- "Great difficulty has been encountered in transferring experienced and skilled men from Southampton to the various dispersal centres owing to the impossibility of obtaining sufficient housing accommodation for them. This has definitely resulted in considerable retardation of production, particularly in Salisbury where it has been definitely impossible to transfer skilled men up to the present."

By June the situation had improved and the Quarterly Report stated:- "difficulty of housing employees is now improving and huts are being built at certain of our dispersal units to relieve this."

By September the Report stated, "provision of huts for employees proceeding and a small number are almost ready for occupation."

In December 1941 the Report stated, "huts for employees making good progress and some are in use in Chandlers Ford."

I feel that the use of the term 'huts' is a bit misleading. They were in fact - and usually referred to as - prefabs, or in other words prefabricated bungalows, and many people lived in them for years after the war was over by which time many had roses round the door!

From all this it can be seen that the story on page 338 of Andrew and Morgan's book, that production was normalised at forty-two per week at the end of October, just four weeks after we were blown up, can only be utter rubbish.

To start with forty-two per week was never our 'norm' and never achieved on a regular basis. Wilf Elliot, during the war, asked me to write up some notes for him about the dispersal and this is what I recorded for him.

"We had delivered our 1,198th Spitfire by the time we were bombed out. (Note. The Quarterly Report to the Board for September stated 1,196. I was going by weekly returns, and weekendings don't always coincide with Quarter endings.) By early 1941, the first stage dispersal was completed and all requisitioned laundries, garages, bus stations, glove factories, steamroller works and strawberry basket factories were producing Spitfire parts and components. The second stage was the building of additional new factory buildings with Ministry sanction. The first stage took six months during which time we produced 350 aircraft whilst completely evacuating factories and offices at Woolston and Itchen to new sites from ten to fifty miles away. By the end of 1941 we had got back to pre-dispersal output and by the middle of 1942 we had passed it."

In other words it took us just over a year ago to get back to our pre-bombing output - not four weeks!

The second stage dispersal was, as detailed in the Quarterly Report to the Board for June 1941 and consisted of further dispersal of the General and Finished Part Stores to Baughhurst and Westbury in Wiltshire, plus the provision of adequate canteen arrangements. In addition the Ministry of Aviation financed the building of new premises at Hungerford, Newbury and Trowbridge, and Machine Tools were installed and in operation at Hungerford by December.

The only other book I have read, that quotes deliveries after the raid, is the one by Alfred Price and that book states that 61 aircraft were delivered in October, 73 in November and 42 in December which gives a total for the last quarter of 1940 of 176, which agrees with my chart.

Looking back on it all I am a bit puzzled as to why Elliot asked me to produce the figures and statement or notes and not Gooch, because at the time I was Sub-Contracts Manager and not Works Manager. Curiously Commander Bird asked me to get out some similar figures for him sometime later. I can only assume that Wilf Elliot had regarded me as his 'general dogsbody' for so long that it had become a habit.

But let us look at those figures on page 338 of Andrew and Morgan's book:-

Week ending 28th September	Output 35
" 5th October	" 32
" 12th October	" 31
" 19th October	" 25
" 26th October	" 42

The figures up to the 19th October seem reasonable - the production at Eastleigh would only be slightly affected by the raid at first, then as time went on and fuselages from Hendy's of Pound Tree Road and Sewards Garage in Winchester Road were slower in being completed due to the dispersal and sorting out of parts output would obviously begin to fall. More so after Hendy's got put out of action by the Southampton blitz at the end of November.

It is therefore highly unlikely that output would suddenly go up by 68% in one week - things just don't work that way.

If the output had 'normalised' at forty-two per week we would have produced over nine hundred aircraft in the following six months, whereas as stated above, we produced about three hundred and fifty - an average of under fifteen per week - which was in the circumstances, extremely good going.

Speaking from memory our lowest weekly output was seven, which I believe coincided with the Southampton blitz when the whole of the town centre was 'taken out' (and Hendy's put out of action) in two six hour raids. Those massive raids on the town affected production almost as much as the raids on the Works. There was a considerable loss of man hours as men tried to patch up their homes or help evacuate their families. The following extract from a letter my wife wrote to my parents after these raids may give some idea of the atmosphere at the time:-

"I cannot tell you what a perfectly ghastly weekend it has been. Saturday evening they started at 6 o'clock and bombed solidly until 2.30am. The whole place seemed to be ablaze. There is hardly anything left of the main street from Plummer's Corner down to the Hythe Ferry - every building in the town centre gone or damaged. The roads out here were a continuous rush of people, some having run half the way. Cars went by in a mad rush for the country. Yesterday the stream of people with suitcases and babies and what they had left was heartbreaking. We took in a mother, baby (Ann's age) and father. They had tramped the streets all day - they were dirty and smelt to high heaven, but it was all we could do! They hadn't had their clothes off for two months and the poor babe was all raw where her clothes had rubbed. I got her a hot bath and found some clothes of Ann's and wrapped her up for the night.

The Jerries came again last night and have now destroyed some more of the town - fires still burning. We have no gas, no water, no light but thank God we have our lives which is all that matters."

The official (Vickers) records of that particular nightmare as contained in the Quarterly Report to the Board for 31st December 1940 stated:-

"<u>Air Raid Damage</u>. During the heavy air attacks on Southampton

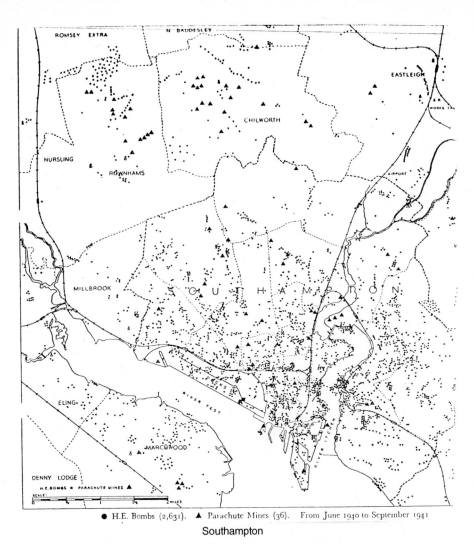

● H.E. Bombs (2,631).   ▲ Parachute Mines (36).   From June 1940 to September 1941

Southampton

on the nights of November 30th and December 1st none of our Dispersal Premises in Southampton suffered any damage whatever, but they were affected for two weeks by the partial failure of electricity supply, gas supply, and the great inconvenience caused by the complete breakdown of telephone communication.

Many of our employees experienced serious hardship due to bomb damage to their houses and difficulties of transport also affected the number of hours which could be worked. During the night of

- 144 -

December 1st a bomb struck the Store Building at the vacated Woolston and also caused a fire which resulted in damage to a considerable amount of material which was stored there."

A very good booklet about the 'Southampton Blitz' written by Tony Brode, describes those two nights of six hour raids as "Southampton's worst weekend." I cannot think of a better description and yet it seems an understatement. There had been 137 people killed of which 96 were killed in their shelters. The number of injured was put at 471 and 1169 properties destroyed and a further 4500 properties damaged.

The fires started on the Saturday night were still burning when the bombers returned on Sunday night in spite of the efforts of the Southampton Fire Brigade reinforced by 160 machines and 2000 men. I believe that so many water mains had been damaged that the water pressure in the hydrants was almost nil. I understood at the time that attempts were made to pump up water from the area of the Town Quay, but the length of hoses involved reduced the pressure and made the idea impracticable. Around 120 aircraft had taken part in the raids dropping some 800 bombs.

We were, at that time, living in Upton Crescent, Nursling, which was about a mile from the outskirts of the town. When you think what our conditions were like you can imagine the absolutely appalling conditions in the town itself. I think it speaks wonders for the guts and tenacity of the men and women that production fell no lower.

Fortunately our dispersal places in Winchester Road and other parts of the town survived although I think some of the premises had to be temporarily evacuated due to unexploded bombs.

I visited Hendy's of Pound Tree Lane the next morning and although it was undamaged there was a gaping hole in the wall between it and Woolworth's next door and also between it and the food store where the fire was still burning and explosions occurring every few minutes, but these turned out to be tins of food exploding with the heat. I vividly remember seeing a huge girder which had been part of 'The Picture House' cinema standing almost vertically in the adjacent park with presumably some ten or fifteen feet buried in the ground. One could only assume that it had been blown high into the air and came down like a javelin.

In January 1941 the 'Powers that Be' began to realise that we were all getting very tired and arrangements were made to try and give us every other Sunday off. It appeared that the Ministry had, at last, come to the conclusion that the Staff were damned nearly worn out - working the hours we did with few proper nights sleep was getting us down, especially as many of us had started the war thoroughly jaded from years of overtime worked in an effort to overcome time lost by the disarmament clots.

From September 1939 the official working hours had been 63 per week for both dayshift and nightshift. In June 1940 the seven day week was started with 70 hours per week dayshift and 73 hours per week nightshift. This killing pace was later, in September 1940, reduced to a 63 hour seven day week for dayshift and a six night 63 hour week for nightshift. The staff were expected to do any hours necessary.

In February my wife was a bit worried about me and in a letter to my parents wrote, "Denis is getting very depressed and seems to think the German Air Force hasn't started yet .... I think Supermarine people are becoming defeatists .... why Heaven knows."

Well - Heaven did know! The Lord knew we were all bloody tired! Apart from that we felt pretty certain that the Germans would start night bombing of towns in a big way having lost the Battle of Britain, and so things turned out.

While we were at the Polygon Hotel I used to nip home for a quick snack occasionally as it was only a few minutes away and once, while doing this, I noticed a lot of men on the side of the road just clear of the town and many were lying in the ditches. I also noticed that some were waving to me and I thought that I recognised some, but was in too much of a hurry to bother about who they were. I learned later that there had been quite a scare amongst our Winchester Road dispersal places due to the completely garbled message about approaching enemy aircraft. I could never quite make out what the final words were which got mangled and spread around, but as far as I could make out the figures for the number of aircraft got transposed, so that fifty aircraft at 500 feet became 500 aircraft at fifty feet!!! As it happened not very long after we had been straffed at Woolston and Itchen our people did not 'wait upon their going' as Shakespeare might have put it, but took off in all directions. The men in the ditches had been trying to indicate that it was advisable for me to join them. I, being completely ignorant of the rumour proceeded on my way just thinking what a nice friendly crowd we had in our Works!

I continued to feel tired. Apart from the long hours I had done before the war and the early part of the war, I think, subconsciously I had worried about the vulnerability of the Works at Woolston and Itchen, the absence of shelters near the Main Works and the galleries around some of the shops which I felt could become death traps. It was not really my responsibility as I was only an Assistant to the Works Manager and not an Assistant Works Manager, but with Elliot away so much I deputised for him and worried in his place. Pratt certainly shared these worries and I think we had done all that we could, but we both had visions of a stick of bombs falling along that road up to the Itchen shelters while thousands of our people struggled to reach them. I mentally cursed those who failed to move us in the thirties.

John Butler who had been our Production Manager and took the responsibility for the output while Elliot was at Castle Bromwich so much was not a very robust man, and not long after we were at the Polygon he had to cease work due to eye trouble and eventually went blind.

Len Gooch, who was the Works Engineer had had little responsibility or any exceptional worries so he and Wilf Elliot who, in spite of problems that Castle Bromwich had, at least had been away from what many of us felt was a prime target which was bound to be blasted to hell at some stage, were comparatively fresh when we got the chop, and just as well!

We were not at the Polygon very long - it was all very makeshift and it was difficult to get any real sort of organisation going - and we were so heartily glad when Hursley Park, a large Country Residence belonging to Sir George Cooper was requisitioned. According to the Quarterly Report to the Board we moved the Office Staff to Hursley Park early in December 1940.

Set in Parkland a few miles out of Winchester we felt considerably safer and set to work to build up a proper and permanent organisation. I went out there with Harry Warren to prepare the way for our office to follow and began to get our files and equipment moved over. We chose two large rooms on the first floor with an inter-communicating door for our offices. Elliot to have one and his secretary Miss George and I to have the other. Later Commander Bird asked if he could join us and Miss George and I graciously gave our permission. Commander Bird was at that time organising the C.R.O. or Civilian Repair Organisation for Spitfires and other aircraft. To have my erstwhile Chief sharing an office with me took some getting used to, but he never 'pulled rank' and we settled into a very comfortable relationship.

* * * * * *

That the strain of those long years of effort and responsibility eventually exacted their toll upon Denis Webb was to be expected, and in the following June his doctor ordered him to rest for a fortnight and he was able to enjoy some time away from the threatened areas with his family and recuperate.

Upon his return he was given the responsibility of organising the Transport Department from the newly based head office at Hursley Park.

That he did this successfully and in his usual 'down to earth' manner he relates in another chapter of this own memoirs, but I feel I shall be encroaching too much on his generosity by telling it here. However, before returning to the factory floor level, I would like to include here for the general reader's benefit extracts from his chapter about the period when he became Sub-Contracts Manager as it reveals a peep behind the scenes at the Management level that the majority of us will be unaware.

The following information extracted from the official Vickers paperwork shows the movement in job titles and descriptions of the Senior Executive that leads up to the Sub-Contract move.

Most major Companies issue an Internal Directory for the use of their Executives, especially if like Vickers their manufacturing and office units are spread across many different locations.

This is the portion of the Vickers Directory appertaining to the Supermarine Works as issued early in 1941 and details the Special Directors (not Main Board directors) and the Executive Officials.

SUPERMARINE WORKS
Administrative and Design Offices.
HURSLEY PARK, WINCHESTER, HAMPSHIRE.
Telephone No: Chandlers Ford 2251
Telegraphic Address: Supermarine, Winchester.
Cost and Wages Offices.
DEEPDENE, MIDANBURY LANE, SOUTHAMPTON.
Telephone No: Southampton 75644

SPECIAL DIRECTORS
Pratt H.B. *General Manager*
Shepherds Crown, Compton Down. Winchester. Twyford 3253
Bird. Sqd-Cmdr, James O.B.E.,R.N.
Park Place, Wickham, Hampshire. Wickham 147

OFFICIALS
Butler. J.F.W. *Production Manager.*
The Brambles, Park Road, Chandlers Ford. Chandlers Ford 2014
Clifton. A.N. *Technical Office*
Netherhill, Awbridge, Nr. Romsey, Hampshire.
Cooper. E. L. *Chief Draughtsman.*
111 Portsmouth Road, Woolston, Southampton.
Southampton 88462.
Dickenson. T.E. *Purchasing*
22 Wilton Gardens, Shirley, Southampton. Southampton 72504
Elliott. W.T. *Works Manager.*
Woolley Green, Braishfield, Nr. Romsey, Hampshire.
Braishfield 281.
Fletcher. W. *Accountant.*
22 Little Lances Hill, Bitterne, Southampton.
Johns. C.W. *Chief Inspector.*
5 Bitterne Way, Southampton. Southampton 3296
Marsh-Hunn. A.E. *Commercial Manager*
The Moorings, Upper Bassett, Southampton. Southampton 68480
Nelson. A. *Assistant Works Manager.*
Hiltonbury, Station Road, Sholing, Southampton.
Smith J. *Design Manager.*
The Oaks, Winchester Road, Chandlers Ford, Hants.
Chandlers Ford 2333.
Webb D. *Assistant Works Manager.*
Beauchief, Romsey Road, Nursling. Rownhams 228.

This Directory has some interesting features. Issued at least four months after the Supermarine bombing and covering mostly the period of initial dispersal it clearly shows the new Head Offices as being established at Hursley Park which was not carried out until either late November or December 1940, that Elliot was Works Manager, with Denis Webb and Arthur Nelson as his two assistants, Butler as Production Manager, and despite the fact that R.J. Mitchell had died in 1937 Joseph Smith was still only designated as Design Manager although he had carried the Senior Design responsibility since R.J.'s death.

The Directory issued in April 1942 showed that Commander Bird had replaced Pratt as General Manager, Elliot had been promoted to the new title of Superintendent, with Gooch now Works Manager, Butler had been deleted due to his unfortunate retirement and really the Works Manager's functions incorporated the previous responsibilities of the Production Manager and was responsible to Elliot, and Denis Webb had become Transport Manager until later that year he was appointed Sub-Contracts Manager.

Joseph Smith eventually became a Special Director and Chief Designer, a well merited change in my opinion which ought post-war to have entitled him to a knighthood.

* * * * * * * * * * * * * * * * *

The circumstances that precipitated Denis Webb into the position of Sub-Contracts's Manager arose through the discovery - quite accidentally - that the person running the Sub-Contract's Department had been the recipient of 'favours' from those subcontractors the Company employed and when one considers that well over half the Spitfire's content was in that category one can understand why some of these 'Goodies' were finding their way into the black market. An internal investigation carried out by the ex Scotland Yard Security Officer to the firm, Jim Wakeling, soon established the facts and the matter was reported to Elliot who took it to Commander Bird.

Their consultation resulted in the offender being removed from his lucrative position and Denis Webb being summoned to Bird's office to face Bird and Elliot asking him to take over the Sub-Contracts Department.

Denis had been around long enough to observe the rather loose organisation and management of this particular department and quite properly showed a reluctance to take the offer on. He was questioned on his apparent reluctance, and as might be expected of a man with his experience told his listeners of what changes he would like to see to make the department function in a manner that would be satisfactory to himself. After a little to-ing and fro-ing all his points were accepted, including the vital one that he should be appointed Sub-Contracts Manager with the authority to deal in the appropriate way with subcontractors who failed to meet the Company's programme of requirements by withdrawing the work from them, and dealing in his own way with those who sought, or maintained, their contracts by what amounted to bribery and corruption.

With these points cleared he handed over the Transport Manager's position to his Deputy and set to with a will to reshape the fresh responsibility.

(Although it has nothing to do with the basic purpose of this book, I can easily identify with Denis Webb's problems when asked to take on the new job. Whilst I was Pre-Production Manager at Hawker Siddeley's Hamble Works I was asked to head a new department that was intended to coordinate all production facilities to be named Production Control. On looking into the detail of the proposition I found that certain elements that I felt were essential to fulfil the objectives required were missing - certain key departments had been omitted that I felt it was necessary to maintain the 'control' element - so I turned it down when the appropriate response was not forthcoming. Later on I was glad I did. Author.)

Denis used all his accumulated knowledge gained during the previous years in staff and management positions of both the Works and Commercial activities to good effect. He adapted some spare space he found available in the upper parts of Hursley House, appointed two assistants to vet the incoming and outgoing mail from the 250 subcontractors who could pass the information on to the appropriate section or refer it back to their Manager if they

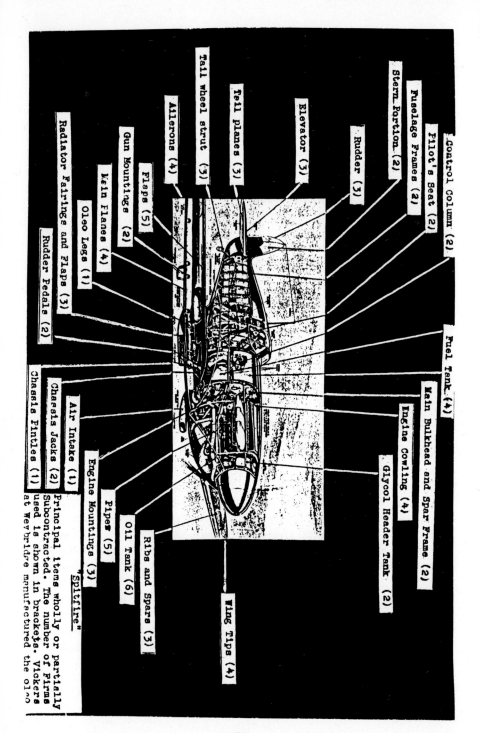

"Spitfire"

Principal items wholly or partially subcontracted. The number of Firms used is shown in brackets. Vickers at Weybridge manufactured the oleo

found anything to query. This method made sure that he was not bogged down all the time with routine paperworks and left time to cogitate for further improvements as well as dealing with the odd awkward customer. When he took over there were some twenty-three men and fourteen women divided into sections controlled by fourteen of the men aligned to the division of the 250 firms dealt with, plus the two assistants and their typist, four more clerks in the records office and his own typist. He had one of his assistants to investigate the work that was spread among the 250 and as a result was able to relocate some of the items to firms already doing similar work and eventually reducing the total number to 136.

The previous incumbent running the department had been in the habit of holding a weekly meeting with his staff to discuss shortages etc., but Denis held just one and then, because they had taken a whole morning as each man was questioned about his particular problems whilst the others had to sit around and doodle on their papers for about two hours for just the fifteen minutes or so they required, he cancelled all future meetings and told them "If you want to talk to me about your problems I will always have time to do so and if I want to talk to you I will come along and see you." He writes, "This went down well as the meetings had obviously wasted their time. However this first and only meeting brought to light various resentments. Instead of Broughton (one of his assistants) signing letters why couldn't they sign their own? I said, "you haven't signed your own before so why should you want to now?" Silence! "If Broughton signs the letters how will the firm know who wrote it and who to speak to?" one asked. "How did they know before?" Again silence. So I said that "Broughton signs for me and reads all the letters so that if there is anything which he thinks should be known by me and out of routine he will pass it to me for signature, this saves me hours of work and gives me more time to sort out our problems, but I will have an alteration done to the Firm's headed paper which will include at the bottom of the page the words' For any query regarding this letter phone Mr......... on extension ....'

Faces brightened all round and that was settled. That first meeting broke the ice and a better atmosphere crept in."

It had been the established custom for the senior management to hold Production Meetings weekly ever since the dispersals had been made. These meetings were of course essential to coordinate the resources where required and for the senior people to know what the state of play was especially as there were so many modifications and different Marks of Spitfires now being produced to keep it in front of various enemy moves. As Sub-Contracts Manager Denis Webb had his contribution to make at these meetings and here I feel it best to let him tell of them in his own words with this extract from his memoirs.

* * * * * * * * * * * * * * * * *

My first appearance at the Weekly Production Meeting which was usually held on a Thursday morning was distinctly nerve wracking as I had only been in the 'hot seat' for a matter of days! The ordeal was further intensified by the way the Conference Tables were arranged! Either deliberately or accidentally the arrangement gave the impression that the Subcontract Manager was being court martialled. The long tables were set in the form of a square and the Chairman (in the first instance Commander Bird), sat in the middle of one table with Elliot on his left and Gooch the Production Manager on his right. On one of the tables set at right angles to them sat the Area Managers, Heaver, Hall, Barby and the Reading man who I think was called Gould. On the other table opposite sat the Chief of Progress Fred Amey, Chief Buyer Tom Dickenson, Chief Inspector Charlie Johns and Ted Gregson who looked after Spares and Embodiment Loan Equipment and John Bull the Chief Planner. At the centre of the fourth table that made up the square sat in lonely state the Subcontracts Manager, which would have given any onlooker the impression that he was up on a charge!

The whole meeting centred round the weekly shortage list prepared by Fred Amey purporting to list all the items which were actually holding up production, or were likely to be very soon. The sole purpose of the meeting appeared to be to pick out those items made by subcontractors and find out what the Subcontracts Manager was doing about it!

I had a list before me extracted from Fred Amey which had been annotated by Broughton with the latest information on deliveries and the expectations of future deliveries, plus information about the reason for hold ups such as enemy action, shortage of materials, etc. As each Area Manager had his say as to how he couldn't produce something, or was behind in his programme because of the bloody subcontractors, Gooch would ask what I was doing about it etc. As the list had dozens of items on it, it took some time to hunt for the answers which - as I had only been in the Department a few days - I could hardly be expected to be *au fait* with!

Jimmy Bird listened for about five minutes and then stopped it. "How can you expect Webb, who has only just taken over the Subcontracts and has been busy getting it organised into new offices, to know all the answers I don't know. What I <u>do</u> know is that in a very short time he will have the answers and you had better make sure of your questions before you ask them!" and with that he looked across at me and grinned. The tone of the meeting changed abruptly.

After I had been on this new job for a few weeks, J.B. stopped me one morning in the main corridor by his office and said, "By the way Webb, you forgot to mention one stipulation about taking on this job." I looked a bit puzzled and he went on, "You never stipulated a rise in salary" and added "But I have fixed one up backdated to the time you took over" and went on his way followed by my thanks.

Having got the men settled in the new offices I started what I called my 'Temperature Chart'. This was designed to show the state of the 'Patient' i.e. the Subcontracts Department. It was a simple graph with the weeks marked off along the bottom and the number of shortages marked off vertically. This Chart hung in my office for all to see. I started this rather simple sort of 'incentive scheme' because I felt the men were all working hard but with no particular sense of achievement - no one had any clear idea as to whether we were winning the production battle or not.

Each Monday, Fred Amey's list came up to me, Broughton would mark the graph and then go round to each of the Staff and make notes about the situation, reason for delays, promises of next deliveries and so on and by Tuesday night would see me with the list. If I was not happy about any particular item I would have a chat with the man concerned and brief myself in more detail and perhaps have a word with the Manager of the Firm concerned and feel fully briefed for the Thursday meeting. By going round the men like that I gradually imbued them with an intense desire to get the Temperature Chart showing a downward curve!

At subsequent Production Meetings, which Elliot sometimes chaired, I had got over 'My first night nerves' and listened very carefully to all that was said even if it did not concern me and I noticed a curious feature! From time to time an Area Manager would mention some item or component in a somewhat quiet voice and I would hear Len Gooch say, "Don't worry about that - it's under control - what have you got on the subcontractors?" I thought, so it isn't only the subcontractors who are holding things up! I soon noticed that even if Fred Amey raised a point about a shortage from our shops he was firmly shut up with the remark, "That's under our control - what have you got on the subcontractors?"

I was rather surprised that Elliot let that sort of thing slide and Bird didn't attend the meeting often enough to latch on. I personally felt that a shortage on our own shops, under our control, was worse than one from our subcontractors. After all, the majority of our dispersal workshops were in nice quiet 'safe' areas whereas many of the subcontractors were working in places like Birmingham, London and other Industrial Areas and were being disturbed by raids. However I kept my views to myself and we just slogged on, but it did occur to me that I was responsible for the coordination of production for 75% of the Spitfire and Len Gooch for only 25% it might be more to the point if I held the Meeting to see how well the rest were making use of the parts my Department was providing! I didn't express these views as I didn't think they would go down very well.

Thanks to the men's efforts that list started to shorten and I think the Department as a whole became more cheerful, but on several occasions men came to me and said, "How can they be short of these things, we're delivering ahead, or on programme?" to which I always replied "Keep at it - I don't give a damn if they get a year ahead of programme! "But it isn't fair - being blamed when we are ahead like that" I told them, "You worry when I blame you for poor deliveries - not when Gooch does." I added, "One of these days they are going to cry wolf too often and I am going to have the intense pleasure in saying "If you are short and want any more delivered you had better order some more we have finished our contracts!" And this did occur on one or two occasions - but due mainly to Planning having slipped up.

I told my lads of my belief in 'removing the excuse'. I said, "Some of the Subcontractors blame their poor deliveries on shortage of parts from us or shortage of materials from us, and you spend hours arguing with them trying to balance deliveries to them against theirs to us, trying to find if any material is still in transit and so on, usually with inconclusive results - don't - if there is any material outstanding or parts, send them and then if they don't deliver on time, clobber them and let them know that if they don't pull their socks up I will cancel their contracts and place the work elsewhere!"

On that basis we continued and the lists shortened even further! Finally it got too short for Len Gooch who asked Ted Gregson if he had all the Spares he wanted. Ted naturally said he could do with more. "Well put them on the shortage list" said Len Gooch!

Up went the 'Temperature Chart' and my men yelled with rage. I said, "Why worry - we've got it down once we can do so again" and added "I think we are calling his bluff!" They entered into the spirit of the game and we got the list down so then Gooch got 'modification sets' added but we got over that as well. Len Gooch soon got more wary of implying that the Subcontractors were to blame for everything but it was not until some time in 1943 that I finally called his bluff.

Commander Bird attended one Meeting and told us all that big things were pending and that we had to make a supreme effort to increase production even further and he wanted us all to go away and think hard during the week about any steps we thought should be taken to boost output and to make the suggestions the following week. I discussed this with my two assistants and we resurrected an analysis chart we had used in the early days which showed the items that came onto the list once in a blue moon, those which came up at very irregular intervals, and those which were fairly regular in their appearance.

They spent a hectic few days going through the list for the last year and about four items showed up as regulars which would need extra to get off the list permanently and so allow increased production to take place. We should obviously have to duplicate some tools and jigs to increase capacity either with the same contractor or some other Firm. The other, more occasional shortages would need some reappraisal but it might be possible to step up their output by increased manpower or extra shifts.

I went down to see Fred Amey and told him what we had done and showed him the results. I suggested he do a similar exercise with the Works items. At first he seemed keen and then said, "But it is all under control!" "But," I said "they are still recurring shortages and unless you can boost output they will stop any increase in production - can you do so without extra tooling and jigging?"

In the end Fred Amey did his analysis and was quite clearly shaken with the result which showed that the Works had about three times as many difficult items than the subcontractors. "God - this is dynamite" he groaned, "I dare not bring this up."

In due course came the Meeting and Bird went round the table asking each Area Manager and Departmental Head for suggestions but not a lot came out. Then he came to me and asked, "What about Subcontracts - have you got any suggestions?" I told him of the analysis we had done and our findings and having read out a short list asked, "With your permission I will get these the jigs and tools for those items duplicated and possibly put on an additional firm which should definitely clear those items."

"Right I agree that" said Bird, and added "Anything else from anyone?" Complete silence and Fred looked awkward and I felt a bit sorry for my old colleague from my apprenticeship days who was clearly worried because Gooch had said nothing about how he was to clear his items! So I thought "To hell with this" and said, "Sir, alongside my analysis Mr Amey has done one for the Works items which should be considered."

There was a momentary stunned hush then Len Gooch became near apoplectic and shouted, "All our stuff is under control and we can deal with it." "Just a minute" said Bird, "I should like to hear Amey's findings" and turning to Fred said "Please read out your list." Poor Fred did so, which showed a much worse situation than mine and Bird said, "Thanks Amey that is a great help." Then addressing the Meeting in general he said, "Unless these items can be produced quicker we can't increase output - are the Area Managers concerned, confident that they can increase their output of those items?"

There was a distinct lack of any sign of anyone willing to stick their neck out! Len Gooch muttered something about being able to cope but Jimmy Bird countered that by asking why, in that case, they were recurring shortages? Then turning to me he said "Webb, I want you to go round the shops making these items and see if you can take them over and put them on a subcontractor, and see me the day after tomorrow and tell me what you intend to do!"

Poor Gooch, I thought he would need hospitalisation! Poor Fred Amey also as I felt sure Len Gooch would half murder him - but he didn't - I think he felt that J.B. might be watching!

When I looked at Amey's list I saw that virtually all the items were made or subassembled in the Southampton Area and I was met with howls of protest from the foremen concerned who reckoned they would have men out of work if I took the items away. It was clear that they just managed to meet the weekly requirements with nothing in hand and could never improve things unless extra jigs and tools were made and more people put on the job. Only about two items were they glad to be rid of and I took them over.

I reported back to J.B. and told him of my findings and he was rather amused and said, "I thought that might be the situation - well - now I know what to do." He did not enlarge on his cryptic remark, but subsequent Meetings became much easier and Len Gooch much less aggressive to the Sub-Contracts Department.

It was after this that the 'supreme effort' called for resulted in us achieving our highest output of the War, reaching an average of thirty-five Spitfires per week for some nine months during the early part of which the Mark X1V began to come off the production line.

But the Meetings occasionally had amusing interludes. I remember that Gregson had once refused to keep quiet about a shortage on our shops and had complained bitterly about lack of certain spares from Newbury and Gooch had extracted a promise from Tom Barby that the parts would be delivered to Ted Gregson by the following meeting. At that Meeting Gregson said he still hadn't received the parts and Tom Barby said that he had quite definitely delivered them to Gregson and after a heated exchange Gooch said that Ted had better get his Department sorted out!

After the meeting I heard Ted and Tom still arguing until - I think it was Fred Amey - joined in and said "Look here Tom, you crafty old blighter, just where were the parts sent to - what was the driver's name, and so on" and at last Tom came out with the truth. He had delivered the parts to Gregson before the meeting by bringing them down in his car that morning and on seeing Ted Gregson's car parked near his had put them in Ted's boot just before going into the meeting!

We all agreed that Tom was a rotten sod and had a good chuckle, and I think it is a measure of the very close friendly relationship that existed between all Departmental Heads that this sort of rather school boyish dirty trick could be played without causing any real bad feeling.

The afternoons after these Weekly Production Meetings used to infuriate the Area Managers , who had plenty of work to do back in their Areas, because Len Gooch expected them to hang around in the corridor outside his office, while he had them in one at a time to discuss various matters. This meant that for a few minutes discussion they had to stand around for a couple of hours at least.

The few minutes discussion always took a long time because it was continually interrupted by telephone calls as he had three telephones on his desk as well as an office intercom set, and frequently endeavoured to use them all at the same time!

I went into his office on one occasion to give him some information and he was holding one phone to one ear and had another cradled between a hunched up shoulder and the other ear whilst he was trying to work the switches of the intercom set with his free hand. This was going on while he was supposed to be having a discussion with Bill Heaver. Bill came over to me and whispered in my ear, "He only needs to shove the other phone up his arse and he would be the picture of efficiency!" I beat a hasty retreat outside!

Why it should have been necessary to go on like that heaven alone knows. Commander Bird in charge of the whole outfit never did and neither did Elliot. It gave me the impression that none of his production people had or were allowed any initiative and had to phone him about everything. The Area Managers had plenty to do without hanging around for hours but I think it was only Tom Barby who let it be known that if Gooch wanted him he could phone him later at his office and carried on with his job. Why Gooch was allowed to carry on like that with such time wasting I have never understood. I never understood either why Elliot allowed the meetings to only discuss shortages from subcontractors. I hardly ever heard anything discussed about our own problems and there must have been plenty. I can only surmise that Gooch was allowed to continue in that way because he was not the Firm's choice of Works Manager (Elliot having already been elevated to the new Superintendent's position. Author.) and so Elliot probably thought that as the all-powerful Beaverbrook people had appointed him he had better be allowed to go on his way. They were a powerful crowd and others seemed to have suffered through upsetting them and so any interference with Gooch might have caused more trouble than it was worth. Commander Bird was the only person to my knowledge to pull him up and point out the error of his ways and that was late in the war. But J.B. was a pretty powerful figure himself and quite definitely not afraid of anyone.

* * * * * * * * * * * * * * * *

In concluding the part extract of Denis Webb's recollections it is only fair to add that he made a resounding success as the Subcontracts Manager including dealing in his own inimitable way with the perennial problem that arises in that particular job of the 'grateful subcontractor' who would "like to show his appreciation and if you could let me have your home address I could send something suitable round for yourself or you wife!" This is an old sore in those positions where contracts and orders are issued from, and no doubt still alive today. Denis' view, and one I share, was that to accept this form of 'bribery' is leaving oneself wide open to future misuse as well as affecting one's ability to cancel any time to suit the Company one is working for, or start laying down the law over late deliveries.

Some Buyers and Subcontract Managers I have personally known blatantly accepted all that was going, but in the main they were eventually mostly exposed and generally left under a cloud. Many years after my Spitfire days I was employed in the Production Management for the Blackburn Buccaneer at Brough where, once the initial order for production quantities was made known a gentleman appeared asking to see me about some machining subcontracting and after an opening discussion about the work and his factory's ability to handle it he suddenly looked across the desk at me and said "I must have this job Mr. Russell" whilst at the same time pushing a rolled-up, elastic banded, quantity of pound notes. My response was to stand up and say to him, "You must excuse me as I have to leave the office for a few moments, but on my

A postwar photograph showing Beverley Shenstone who was very largely responsible for the successful design of the Spitfire wing. Centre and second from right Denis Webb when Deputy Service Manager.   Source Webb.

return I shall not expect to see you or 'that' still here." He'd gone when I returned and so had the bankroll, and of course he never got any work from the Company.

Reverting to Denis Webb once more he eventually was put in charge of the Experimental flying, first at High Post when that was developed and then at Chilbolton until that closed down. He was then transferred to the Weybridge Headquarters for the Vickers Group and concluded his working life as Special Assistant to one of the Directors. He is the only person I have known who spent the whole of his working life in the service of the one Company and I am glad that he is still enjoying his well earned retirement years and still able to bring his remarkable memory and documents to aid this struggling author.

Chapter Seven - From my Postbag

From what has already been told it is obvious that the dispersal of the main Woolston and Itchen Works was a major upheaval for all who had worked at either of these two sites.

The Southampton Area under the direct control of Arthur Nelson continued to be the main supplier of completed Spitfires throughout the remainder of the war from those units under Supermarine's control.

Eastleigh airport remained the finals and flight centre for the area with almost no interference from the enemy. Fuselages were assembled as in 'K' shop on the ground floor at Sewards in Winchester Road and the upper floor became the 'out of jig' installation prior to the fuselage being transported to Eastleigh. Across the road from them the Wings were being built in Hants and Dorset's bus garage, whilst detail manufacture similar to the old Woolston 'F' shop was carried on under the auspices of an ex 'F' shop chargehand, Syd Bloxham, Hendy's down in the town suffered a while during the night blitzes but still managed to add its quota to the fuselage building for all of the war.

A machine and toolroom facility was set up in Lowther's Garage at Shirley and the then precious, and only, Jig Borer the company had was safely ensconced in its temperature controlled cabin there with other machines supervised by Dick Earl.

I have to hand a letter about Lowthers sent to me from America by Eric Ranwell who was an apprentice there at the time. He writes.

"Lowthers was on Park Street or Road and I was on the first or second row of the lathes, ahead of me were the usual admin. offices. On the right, a little ahead, was the grinding machine, to the right of that was a wall, brick I think. I recall that wall when two of us would go to climb the iron stairs to the roof to watch the Doodle Bugs. When the engine cut out you never saw such a rush back down.

"Over on the left more Lathe type machines and Capstans. I would be roughly in the centre, behind me more machines, possibly shapers, and one large Jig-boring machine enclosed in its own brick, temperature controlled area and operated by one designated operator. I was surprised to note that practically all the big machines were American, Cincinattis, etc. and a couple of German ones. Further over on the right was a space where the tea urns used to stop for our morning cuppa at the back of this a nurses station completely enclosed, and to the right of this station and forward, were the Pattern making areas, benches, saws, shapers, and two or three flywheel presses, and further on an Inspection area. I well remember this Inspector, a Scot, who kindly gave me a very nice six inch slide rule in its own leather case. I liked the Pattern shop, more I think than the other apprentices. I suppose I was not that good with the big machines but the first tool I made when put on to the fly press, and an aluminium sheet slid in and the press operated to everyone's surprise it was passed as well within tolerances.

"One day I was on a Lathe turning a huge bar of Magnesium - the

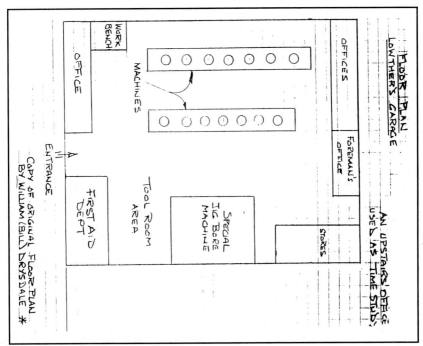

Floor plan Lowther's Garage Copy of original floor plan by William (Bill) Drysdale

- 165 -

cut was at least 1/8th to 3/16th of an inch thick and the slurry was flowing fast when suddenly I heard the chargehand, Sam, say in my ear, "Stop the lathe and don't move!" I did as I was told and apparently the magnesium cut-away waste had wrapped around me and would have cut me to pieces had I moved. They got wire cutters to cut me loose and afterwards instructed me to use a rod to guide the cut away."

Eric has kindly enclosed a rough sketch of the shop's layout as best he can recall it abut I have included another for the reader's benefit. It must also be remembered that if he was looking for doodle bugs it must have been in the 1944/45 era, and no doubt a lot more modern machinery has been imported and established well after the early dispersal days of 1940. Nevertheless it is help-ful to have this insider view of one unit of the many that I had no personal experience of visiting. The reader may be pleased to know that later Eric went on to Supermarines Design Office staff and when the works closed, after the war he eventually went to America where he worked on the Design staff of Boeing/Vertol until his retirement a couple of years back.

Right from its earliest days Lowthers played an important role in providing a large part of the jigs and tools that were required for the expanded production that was needed and met by the newly formed 'country' areas, as well as meeting the requirements that never ceased as the design changes emanated from the Hursley Design team that was essential to keep pace with the improved aircraft types that the Germans were making.

Later the Southampton Area extended itself to Chandlers Ford where it took over a commandeered agricultural machines show-room, and to Winchester where two garages were requisitioned, Shorts as another machine shop and Chiswells as a detail and minor sub-assembly unit under the watchful eye of one of the best sheetmetal workers I ever knew, Fred Bristowe of ex 'P' shop at Woolston.

The increased production that gradually evolved as a result of these moves (see the production chart graph and the accompanying graph showing the increase of personnel) soon demanded more space at Eastleigh and whereas at the beginning of the war Supermarines

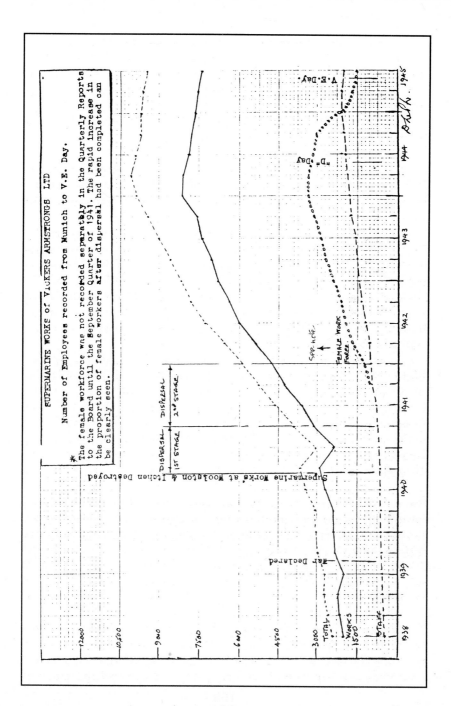

SUPERMARINE WORKS OF VICKERS ARMSTRONGS LTD

Number of Employees recorded from Munich to V.E. Day.

* The female workforce was not recorded separately in the Quarterly Reports
to the Board until the September Quarter of 1941. The rapid increase in
the proportion of female workers after dispersal had been completed can
be clearly seen.

Supermarine Aviation Works of Vickers Armstrong Ltd.
Employees at latter end of 1940

The dip in the number of employees just before War broke out was due to the Call Up of all Reservists. When we asked for the Release of key men, they were returned to us.

The big loss of man power immediately after the destruction of the Works was, of course due to our inability to employ them until the requisitioned premises had been taken over and made ready for use.

The Quarterly Report to the Board for December 1940 reported:

"The continuity of production at Southampton has been seriously affected by the results of the bombing attack on Woolston and Itchen Works on September 26th.

The dispersal of production was proceeded with immediately but temporarily the number of employees was considerably reduced and a considerable proportion were engaged for several weeks on salvage work.

The number of employees at the time of the enemy action on September 26th and at the end of the succeeding months is given below:

	Works	Staff	Total
September 26th	2,002	668	3,660
October	2,497	656	3,153
November	2,453	670	3,123
December	2,407	672	3,079

The number of employees is now being steadily increased at the various dispersal units and as far as possible, labour already resident in the dispersal areas is being taken on, particularly women and unskilled men for training".

had the hiring of one and part of another of the main three hangars there (ex first world war American Navy build) it now became
essential, after a short spell of utilising Worthy Down aerodrome
for finals and flight, to occupy the remainder of the second hangar
and enclose the space between the two so that that as well became
part of the facility. That alteration remained operative until the
main move was made by Supermarine's to South Marston long
after the war and saw the building of wings for both Swift and
Scimitar aircraft.

A further addition to the original Southampton dispersal sites came
about when Carey and Lambert's Austin House showrooms were
requisitioned and I understand became Southampton's supplier
of Leading Edge Assemblies for the wings.

There were many and differing Stores units set up in all sorts of
out of the way places of which I was very unaware and I have
omitted them as very little useful information is now available.

As may be imagined the race against time to set up the 'country'
Areas, at Salisbury, Newbury, Reading and Trowbridge was geared
to what they were making.

Trowbridge and Salisbury areas I have covered during the times I
was personally there and mentioned the improved facilities that
were erected after 1942.

One Area that I had very little knowledge of was Newbury, apart
from the fact that my ex-lodger companion Duxbury had been
moved there when the wheeling squad had been split from our
Chandlers Ford base.

The Newbury Area under the managership of Tom Barby was different from most others as it did not produce complete Spitfires,
but what it did, and did remarkably well, was to supply initially
fairly small parts and sub-assemblies, and then after the Shaw
Works and the Hungerford machine shop was built provided probably the bulk of each area's machined and specially formed
(drawbench and rubber press) parts.

Through the good offices of Lawrence Cummins, Editor and Direc-

A Newbury Sports Day presentation by Tom Barby (third from right) Source. Stan Brown

tor of the Newbury Weekly News Group, I heard from a number of people who filled the gap in my knowledge and in many cases supplied interesting information about their own experiences and others who worked at these factories and in some cases sent me some of their photographs to use.

As in all the other dispersed units, the initial properties requisitioned were mainly garages or car showrooms. Newbury began its Spitfire life in Stradlings, Nias's, and the Thames Valley Bus garages and one of my correspondents, Mrs Doris Drewitt wrote of how she was given some training at the Technical Training College at Wolverton in Buckinghamshire before finding herself three or four months later returned to Newbury and Nias where space was very cramped. Later she was moved to Mill Lane and it was there that she met and worked with Hilton Duxbury and it was from her I learned that he had died. One of the items on which she worked was the pilot's seat. Mill Lane was the location of the Thames Bus Garage.

A Spitfire at a 'Victory Parade' float at Newbury. Source. Anon.

Another person who preferred to remain anonymous mentions that he joined Vickers as soon as they appeared in Newbury in 1940, working first in Stradlings in West Street on assembly work then later at Passes (?) where the embryo of the machine shop had been formed. He also sent the photograph of a Spitfire mock-up on a carnival float at the end of the war.

Mrs. Dorothy Cooper very kindly wrote of her days at Newbury from 1941 to 1945 telling me that she too began at Nias Garage - which she informs me is now part of the Kennett Centre - and that Passe's was another garage nearby which was used as a processing unit (salt baths etc.) for some of the forming operations required at Nias"s. She made countersunk washers and took up welding. One of the curious sidelights of those days occurs in her letter and I quote, "I loved the work and earned quite a lot of bonus. The hours were long from 8 until 8 dayshift, also nightshift, I was interested in tool-making and there was a discussion to see if I would be able to do this job if trained. The 'powers that be' decided that as I was a young bride with a young husband in the Army stationed at home this would be decidedly risky from their point of view as I might become pregnant. As a new factory was being built in Mill Lane in Newbury most of the girls were moved and I was left at Nias while they decided what should happen to

Staff at Mill Lane, Newbury. Source Stan Brown.

me because another factory was being built at Shaw on the outskirts of Newbury. We had lots of repair work to do on the ejector seat button and worked overtime for a few weeks while the work was sent out to planes overseas. I remember soldering the wires which splayed out if too much heat was applied. I remember also the wife of Mitchell, the Designer, coming round the factory one day and she talked to me.

"When most of the men were moved to Shaw I went with them as chargehand of dayshift. There were over a hundred girls, mostly part-timers, from all walks of life. There were huge machines which mostly came from America; the noise was indescribable and I suffered from nosebleeds etc. until I got used to it and stayed until my husband left the Army in 1945.

"While at Nias, Newbury was bombed by a runaway plane. I happened to have that day off but my mates told me that the factory was strafed with bullets and one bomb was buried near the factory and did not explode. I remember going to have a look at this bomb next day guarded by police.

"Nightshift was worst, and I remember walking round the benches seeing girls drilling holes almost asleep. There was one girl whose hair was caught in the conveyor belt bands between the wheels and she was almost scalped. We had to wear scarves to keep our hair in place. There were guards on machinery that was considered dangerous so special checks were made on those who took them off to do the job more quickly."

The bombing that Dorothy Cooper refers to happened at 4.35pm on Wednesday, February 10th, 1943, was quite destructive on a small town community like Newbury as apparently a lone Dornier bomber loosed eight

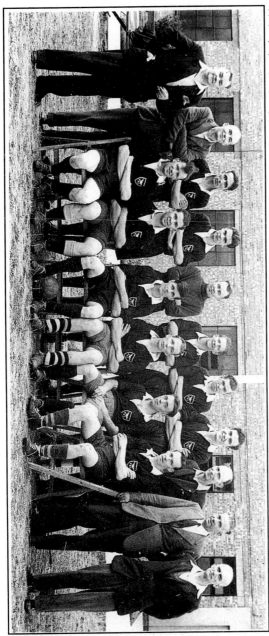

Vickers Newbury football team. Hilton Duxbury sitting front left. Source. Stan Brown.

high explosive bombs on the town's southern side, killing fifteen people and injuring dozens more, apart from the destruction to school, church and a number of dwellings. According to the Newbury Weekly News Supplement that was sent me this was not the only experience of enemy attack but was by far the most catastrophic. Other information from the same source, and published after the war, stated that flying bombs (V1's) at Shaw and Combe causing little damage and fortunately no casualties landed on June 27th and July 12th 1944. This must surely be one of the deepest penetrations made!

Further news of the Newbury Area came from some of the ex-Supermarine personnel who had been drafted there during the main dispersal, mostly from members of the old 'F' shop at Woolston, and both Stan Brown and Roy Maidment have kindly loaned me photographs of the period. Roy was an apprentice at

A group of 'F' shop lads in happier days. Taffy Edwards of Progress second from right at back, and Bob Culley who was dispersed to Trowbridge later on left kneeling. Stan Brown.

The pedestrian bridge west of Woolston railway station on which was based a Bofor's gun. Some of our casualties occured when fleeing employees sought shelter under it.   Author

the same time as myself and he recalls the names of some of our contemporaries such as; Bert Franks, Wally Lambert, Frank Feltham, Harry Brown, Frank Wadley, Ron Wilkinson, Les, Ted and Jack Diaper and many others which I'm sure will be of interest to their sons and daughters and even, as in my own case, our grandchildren.

Roy Maidment gives an account of the Woolston raid in his letter which adds to our first hand knowledge of that day. It reads as follows: "On Thursday, the 26th, you will remember we had plenty of warning. Some of us were kicking a ball about when it started. Some went into an alcove in the railway embankment (this is at the Woolston end) and they got a direct hit and all died. Myself and four others managed to get into an Anderson shelter in an empty house garden opposite the works. After the raid we went to the embankment, but it was hopeless to try and get anybody out. The Bofor ack-ack gun crew who were stationed above the railway line gave a good account of themselves."

Those readers who have read 'Spitfire Odyssey' may recall that the bridge over the line with the Bofors crew on it was until the Tuesday and Thursday raids my own viewing spot. Lady Luck had not deserted me, thank goodness!

In his letters Roy also mentioned that he too had gone to the Itchen Works bombed area on the Tuesday and had seen bodies being laid out in front of the factory; adding that he lost a pal, Alfie Petts, there and mentioned the one female fatality, Peggy Moon.

Prior to his move to Newbury - and after the bombing - he says:- "I went to Salisbury in January 1941, our job was to connect and check datum locations and jig points on various jigs. I was at Anna Valley garage for about two weeks where they were making rear fuselages and tailplane units. I then spent the next five weeks at the Wessex unit where the main fuselages were to be made. At that time I was not involved with production, but the jigs and fixtures. Then back to Lowthers which was a machine shop and tool room until December 1942 when I was transferred to Newbury.

"The Newbury Area at that time was comprised of five units; Nias, Pass and Stradlings were all ex-garages, Mill Lane which had been a former bus station and about eight miles away was the Hungerford Unit which was a purpose-built factory making machined components with the ex-Supermarine Works Assistant Foreman, Mark Webster in charge. Stradlings was the same as Lowthers in Southampton, a machine shop and toolroom, Pass was sheetmetal components treatments and painting shop. Nias was detail fittings and template making, and Mill Lane was airframes, bulkheads etc: In August 1943 Shaw Works was opened. This was purpose-built with a machine shop, tool room, detail fitting, sub assembly, press shop, pattern shop, a small foundry, also a Process shop where they did anodising, cadmium, heat Treatment salt baths and a degreasing bath. So after August 1943 Stradlings, Nias and Pass were closed and the Newbury Area consisted of the Shaw work, Mill Lane and Hungerford. It stayed like this until 1946 when Mill Lane and Hungerford were closed - their work, now much reduced, transferred to Shaw works until that finally closed in 1959 when everything was transferred to the SouthMarston Works at Swindon.

The people employed in the Newbury Area during the war totalled

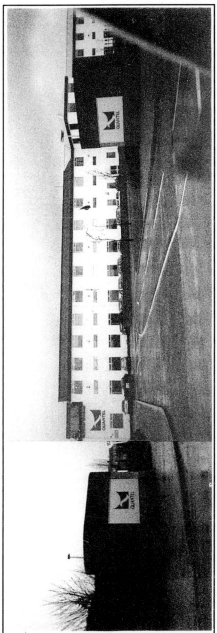

The Shaw Works factory, Newbury as it is in 1994. Source Hamblin

about 500. We even had a coachload of girls from Scotland and another from Wales. The people that came from South-ampton I would think was about 100.

"I think the people of Newbury will always remember Vickers as one day someone inadvert-ently tipped cyanide down the drain and killed all the fish in the Kennet-Avon canal between Newbury and Reading. This caused a hell of a row and the Company was fined over it."

Roy Maidment remained with Vickers, transferring to South Marston in the move there but not before he married his wife Eve who used to work in the Ratefixing Office with Arthur Baker, Bill Hillier and Arthur Pannell, retiring in 1982 after 46 years with the Company. They now live in St. Ives, Corn-wall, and celebrate their Golden Wedding next year.

Another contributor is Frank Hamblin. He came to the Com-pany straight from school (Newbury Grammar School), was interviewed first at Nias Garage in 1943 by Frank Cham who used to be the Foreman of Woolston's 'F' shop and started his career at the newly opened Shaw factory where he was given some of the normal mun-

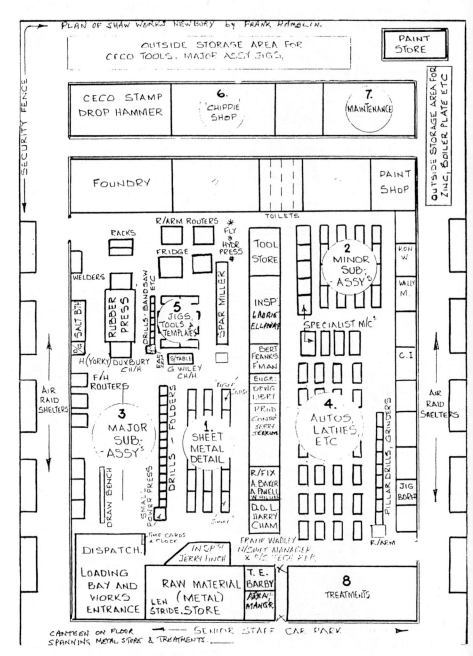

Plan of Shaw Works, Newbury by Frank Hamblin.

dane jobs that young new starters experienced like removing tooling lugs from formed items, in his case a Spitfire intercostal, with an antiquated set of bench shears - much to his apparent disgust! Later he progressed on to making No. 8 templates, No. 1 clapper blank tools, No. 3 nest pierce tools, No. 4 Folder blocks and 11A's Pierce and blank tools, which were the basic tool numbers at the time, and continuing in tooling of various types until he left in 1953. His enthusiasm, born in those boyhood days, has never left him and he spent most of the remainder of his working life in Aviation Industry apart from his National Service days in the R.A.F. in 1946. Fortunately he has a retentive memory and has supplied the layout drawings of the Shaw Works herewith, as well as the photograph of Shaw Works as it is today.

Even if Newbury did not have the finals and flight facilities that the other areas had it has every right to be justifiably proud of its contribution to the Spitfire's wartime production.

The Reading dispersal followed a similar pattern to that of both Salisbury and Southampton and had its aerodrome facilities via Henley and the R.A.F. aerodrome at Aldermaston.

The requisitioning of Vincents garage became their fuselage production unit, and the Great Western garage provided the space for wing jigs and associated assemblies. Later, this capacity was increased by the purpose built Caversham factory. The time scales for these movements were also very close to the other areas mentioned for their set up and production commencement. The Area Manager at the beginning was Ken Scales who had been the flight shed foreman at Eastleigh but he was replaced later by Ron Gould following some irregularities being uncovered over the usage of petrol.

Most of the correspondence I received about Reading unfortunately only repeated much the same sort of story as has already been told about the other units and no useful purpose would be served by their repetition.

One elderly lady, Mrs. Kellaway, wrote that both her brother and husband had been at the Woolston factory when it was bombed and following their eventual transfer to Reading she too took up

Vincents, Reading Area unit showing detail fitting and fuselage assembly work in progress. Vickers/CUL.

employment at Vincents garage on frames for the fuselages. Another, Mrs Margaret Lawrence, wrote that she worked at Markhams in the Caversham Road. This apparently may well have been one of our multitude of subcontractors as apart from making fuel tanks, and at home, canvas back rests and head rests for Spitfires the firm was also making 14ft long fuel tanks for the Wellington.

The Reading Area closed down somewhat quicker than others, for one thing the R.A.F. wanted the return of Aldermaston - as at Keevil - and the products of the area's various units were absorbed back into those units that Vickers only intended to retain for the completion of foreshortened and cancelled contracts they held, and for the new development work on which they were then engaged. Eventually the whole Supermarine organisation ended up at the South Marston factory near Swindon where it finally expired in a very sad manner - but that is another story.

(To avoid any misunderstanding, the Spitfire did not have an ejector seat, and I'm sure this is a genuine mistake in Dorothy Cooper's letter C.R.R.)

It will be remembered that earlier Sqdr. Commander Bird's return to Supermarines at the outbreak of war was used first to set up a Civilian Repair Organisation for the Spitfires 'out in the field' from appropriately knowledgeable persons within the Southampton works.

Very little has been written or said about these men, and unfortunately now very few of them remain to tell their tales. Conversely, fortunately for me I have still retained contact with one so engaged even though he lives 14,000 miles away in Queensland, Australia. When I mentioned this he replied with the usual enthusiasm that most of my correspondents reveal when asked to relate their Spitfire days. Although this is only one man's experiences I will cover most of his account in his own words. His name is Jim Mole.

"Since trying to think of those days for you I have found myself going back to 1937 and Woolston days, remembering lots of names that I had really forgotten about - Ted Henry, Bert Rainbow, Charlie Mathews and many more. It was funny that after the Woolston bombing you and I never came together again until the early 50's at Itchen."

"After the bombing I went to Hursley for a while and then went on to outstation work until the war ended. Do you remember a riveters mate called Joe Gallon who they reckoned could carry a Spitfire radiator under one arm? He was really a big fellow and quite a character as I recall who was mainly on the wings section at Woolston. Earlier in 1940 a team was sent out to modify Mk. 5A Spitfires which only had one cannon in each wing to Mk. 5B's which included two Browning machine guns in each wing. We worked on the operational aircraft in Morris's at Oxford. Some of the men who were there with me and who you might remember were Len Talbot, Mike Wrapson and Tom Rodd."

Jim Mole of the Outstation and Repair organisation now retired to Australia. Source J. Mole.

"Immediately after the bombing I did a spell at Sunlight Laundry in Winchester Road until I was selected by Bert Diaper to be one of the first few 'bods' to start the Experimental Department at Hursley in an old garage at the back of the house. As I recall there were two detail fitters, two sheetmetal workers, and a machinist on a shaper. We used to travel daily backwards and forwards to work in an old bus we called 'the Yellow Peril' driven by Mr. Jones. Of course this old bus was replaced after a while when more workers came in to the newly built Exp Hangar at the road end of the Hursley House drive."

In a subsequent letter, having asked him for further details, Jim wrote:- "You were asking what and where Morris's of Oxford was. It was a part of Nuffields's Morris Motor Works at Cowley and part of it had been turned over into a repair unit for badly damaged Spits. that had to have fuselages re-jigged. They did the wings as well. These were reassembled and test flown from a large field at the back of this big workshop. Alex Henshaw was the test pilot and he also flew the ones we modified."

"Your other query regarding Sunlight Laundry. There were no wings there as the ceilings were too low. I was there on sub-assemblies and details; there was also a girls section but I can't remember their chargehand - it could well have been Chris Parker and the girls from the old 'P' shop balcony. The foreman there was Mr. Bloxham (known as 'old Blocks' by us lads) and our chargehand was Bert Diaper and it was from here that Bert collected six of us to start the Experimental section at Hursley, probably early in 1941. I was there when they built the new hangar and I was only in the new building for a few months when Don Kirkwood and I applied for an outside 'reps' job."

"I wouldn't have missed the outside reps job for worlds as it was very interesting and the enclosed leaflets on Ibsley Airfield you sent me was like reliving old times. I meant to tell you in my last letter that 'The First of the Few' was partly filmed at Ibsley and they borrowed a Spitfire we had lined up for an undercarriage repair - it had made a belly landing - but before we could get it off the field they placed explosive charges in sandbags around it to make it look like a crash landing. Of course another 'Spit' flew over the site and the film was cut at that, then a shot was taken as the explosive charges blew whilst the 'Spit' was on the ground. All very realistic, but where we would have just had an undercart repair we now had the problem of changing lots of ballraces that were full up with sand. I don't think they had sealed ballraces in those days. It Wouldn't have been so bad if the silly 'b's' had closed the hood over the cockpit which was smothered in the stuff."

So with those few words one can see that life in the Repairs Organisation had its lighter moments, my only regret is that there is nothing more I can add to a side of the Spitfire story that remains largely untold.

Chapter Eight - Until the Peace

Somewhat to my surprise, and I must add to my personal relief from a set of domestic circumstances that had almost overwhelmed me, I was requested by my Area Manager, my ex-foreman, Bill Heaver, to consider a return to Trowbridge where a new, and purpose-built hangar, had been erected whilst I had been at Salisbury at Keevil aerodrome. I jumped at the opportunity and at the end of August 1943 I duly presented myself to Vernon Hall, the Area Manager, at his newly built headquarters and factory in the Bradley Road. Once the formalities of transfer had been observed and arrangements for lodgings settled I caught the following morning's transport - a canvas covered lorry - at the most convenient pick-up point for the five mile drive to the aerodrome and Archie Preskett the unit's foreman.

After the restrictions on space and other facilities which had been the High Post lot Keevil was a palace. Large enough to allow six Spitfires down each side, and with sufficient space between them to allow ample room to manoeuvre a Coles crane it spelled the end of the "All under the wings" cry and the backbreaking lift that it had entailed.

The hangar had only been operative for a few weeks, its first delivery of JF 900, a Mark 8, was only made on August 21st and as I soon found I was not alone in being seconded here from High Post as its 'hard-core' of experienced employees gathered to become the hundred or so that eventually fully staffed the unit. Nobby Clark, the painter, Hilda Henry our fillet fitter and compass swinger and Vic Woodgate the hydraulics man, as well as Jack Lansom from some other area had joined in.

Although the work was mostly on Mark 8 and 9's and later Mark 14's, it differed only in small detail to that we had done before and therefore the settling in period was much reduced and now that the new Bradley Road factory was making its own wings and fuselages it was only a very short time before we were operating a full nightshift on a month on, month off basis. Archie Preskett our foreman, had been at Eastleigh from way back in the early Spitfire days - I think he may have been there during the prototypes days

Keevil Hangar personnel. Seated under propellor boss Archie Preskett the Foreman. Vickers.

The Supermarine Hangar beside the R.A.F. Airfield at Keevil near Trowbridge.   Vickers.

- and consequently he knew the aircraft inside out, but what impressed me most was his quiet, authoritative way in which he treated his staff and any aircraft problems that might arise. Archie was a gentleman and the example he set rubbed off on to most of his staff making Keevil a most happy shop in which to work.

As the numbers built up from the trawl that the Ministry of Labour had operating under the scheme for 'directed' labour it was considered quite ordinary to hear the singsong lilt of Wales, alongside the harsher twang of the Northern counties and the softer 'burr' of those from the West Country and even our own Hampshire.

There were never any disputes - certainly not to my knowledge - and there was a genuine desire to pitch in to whatever work was offered whether it be strictly in ones trade category or not. From a personal point of view I was inducted into the mysteries of the hydraulic system, the alignment of cannons and not least, how a compass swing was accomplished and the meaning of the deviation cards.

Our hangar was set beside an R.A.F. aerodrome, an operational one, and day after day we would see the giant Short Stirling bombers set out for their bombing trips to France, or the United States Thunderbolt squadron set off for its long range fighter cover for bombers from elsewhere.

We sheetmetal workers, six in all, formed three teams of two, and with the benign agreement of our foreman arranged our workload so that two teams were always on dayshift, because that was when flight attendance was required, and one shift on nights. This worked very well, we even found the occasional time to spare when our efforts could assist some other part of the routine, e.g. compass swinging, hydraulics, and lest we be cast in the mould of saints let it be said that there were also a few petrol cigarette lighters made.

It seems invidious to pick out individuals in such a happy shop, but it is fair to mention that our First Aid post 'nurse' was an ex-ballet dancer, a 'fitter' was a chap that had been buried alive for some hours during the Bristol blitz, and our nightshift chargehand had been a mechanic for a travelling fairground.

With this great diversity of labour, not only at Keevil but also even more marked at the much larger Bradley Road factory, as well as the minor units that still operated like Southwick and Hilperton, there was inevitably in the wartime conditions certain problems that arose.

On one hand there were young women of eighteen or so freed for the first time in their lives from the protective care (or smothering as some considered it) of their parents and mixing for the first time in close proximity with older women and young and old men. There were also many young, often recently married, women whose husbands or boyfriends had been called up for military service and most probably sent abroad. We also had a few actual prostitutes who were not averse to working hard building Spitfires during the day then plying their other trade - mostly with the Americans? - at night.

On the other hand there were many men separated from their families by Government 'direction of labour', some who openly admitted their delight, and a lot of young men who generally for reasons of either failing the call-up medical or the "Essential services' being in a restricted occupation, and here and there, although not so blatant as today, the odd homosexual.

There was also the predatory female landlady, which I can vouch for personally on two occasions, one at Salisbury and the other at Trowbridge, but which I managed to escape because of the inherent difficulties that might arise from the husband's continued residence.

What with all that; the natural forces that influence our lives and the blackout, it was not surprising that a number of illicit liaisons intruded on our war work, adding in some instances that indefinable spice occasioned when 'playing with fire.'

At the Keevil Hangar we had proper canteen facilities, as had the new Bradley Road Works, which were a far cry from the makeshift canteen in a portion of Knee's, the local furniture emporium, storage room, and infinitely better than the long cold walk we had had to endure in the winter to reach the requisitioned flying club house at High Post, or the adaptation that the Salisbury Assembly Room had served for those at Wessex, Anna Valley or Wilts and Dorset.

Entertainment was a problem at Salisbury - the two cinemas and the local pubs being nearly all that was available - but there we had created our own concert party which had served us well. Not long after I had returned to Trowbridge two floors of the largest store in the city - then known as Style and Gerrish, now Debenhams - were taken over by the Ministry of Labour and made into a recreational facility for War workers which must have helped a lot.

The concert party idea we carried on to Keevil and eventually amalgamated with another group trying to establish the same idea at Bradley Road which worked out extremely well as the canteen at Bradley Road was quite large and had a stage and backstage facilities. Here we managed to entertain our fellow workers, made a Works Wonders broadcast on the BBC, and later were encouraged and helped by the Ministry of Labour to take our show to the surrounding areas by their providing the coaches for transportation to as far as Corsham and other locations.

By this time the country had been four years at war and a certain degree of war weariness was becoming apparent. Larger war works had had the benefit of professional entertainers and shows being put on for them, but our relatively tiny and widely spread units hardly qualified for such luxuries.

One magnificent boost in the Trowbridge Area was the purpose-built War Workers Recreational Centre that was built on the edge of the town. It had bathrooms which, in Trowbridge, were a god-send to the majority of us in lodgings. Staffed by a paid Warden under Ministry of Labour auspices and run by a committee from the area's factories, this centre served as a meeting place among colleagues without the aid of alcoholic beverages which at that time was getting harder and harder to locate. Fortunately at Bradley Road one of the Time Office staff was also the Landlord of one of the town's 50-odd Pubs and we relied on 'Old Fitz' to keep us informed on the erratic timings for alcoholic deliveries.

Everyone in the Country was, by this time, keyed up by the eagerly awaited invasion of Europe. We, at the Spitfire factories knew that large numbers of our products would be required to assist in that great venture, just as we had known how vital its role had been in Malta and the invasion of Sicily.

Right outside of the Keevil hangar we began to notice the build-up. Albermarle aircraft arrived and gliders of various types to be towed by them and the Stirlings.

When attending compass swinging or acting on stand-by during a Spitfire's test flight they were in clear view through the large gap in the separating hedge between us and the R.A.F. station proper, and it was the R.A.F.'s runways and perimeter tracks that our pilots used for their takeoffs and landings.

It was my good fortune to be there the night that the massed gaggles of aircraft and gliders set forth into Europe and to see them with all their identification lights on; a sight that had not been seen for over four years.

The success of the landings, the gradual pushing of the enemy back towards his own land provided just the stimulant we needed to increase our efforts to give something of ourselves to the final outcome.

It was becoming obvious, even to the uninitiated, that the Spitfire had reached the limit of its design capabilities. For all those years, from 1936 onwards, it had been subjected to the designer's genius to extend its front line fighter role, and they had succeeded magnificently, but there had to be a limit and my first intimation of its intended successor came when I was transferred to the Bradley Road factory where the tail end of the new 'Spiteful' was to be built.

It is a matter of history that this aircraft's conception was overtaken by the development of the jet, but before that took place a few were built and its new laminar type wing served to suit Supermarines first jet aircraft.

On VE day I heard the news from an excited bevy of nurses in the local cottage hospital having just undergone surgery for a stomach problem and then, it was only a few short months before the atomic bomb put an end to hostilities world wide.

The Spitfire production era was over. Gradually requisitioned premises were returned to their original owners and their staffs dispersed back to their homes. In the new factories, like Bradley Road and the one built off Salisbury's Castle Road after I had left, the employees who could be shed were allowed to go home, while a dwindling few carried on until our fates were decided for us. Some who had met, married and settled in their areas decided to stay on and in a number of cases, are still there to this day.

Others, like myself, who had no real urgent call to return to Southampton, remained until the future plans for the reconstitution of Supermarines could be decided and when that came to fruition the Bradley Road factory remained for some years as a part of the South Marston works area and the location of the Company's Head Office. The Itchen factory was rebuilt, the Flight Testing Centre that had been established under Jeffrey Quill alongside the old flying club hangar at High Post in 1944 was switched to the better runway facility at Chilbolton, near Stockbridge, and the last vestige of Spitfires was centred on Eastleigh where the 'surplus to requirement' Spitfires were repurchased by the Company and refurbished to meet the requirements of interested foreign powers, which included an adaptation for some of a two-seater version.

Once the Spiteful contract had ceased and various other changes were being made I returned to Eastleigh where apart from making Spitfire spares, mostly cowling panels and fillets, I found myself making the skins for the Vickers Viking passenger airliner. Twice I was sent back to Trowbridge for short stays on work that they thought I was required for, but by now an unsettled feeling had come into my life and later in July 1947, I decided it was time for a change. My last job was to wheel a set of Spitfire side cowling panels. I must confess that I left with a heavy heart and yet certain that in my small way I had shared a precious piece of history. I can only hope that this account reflects something of the way all the other areas and employees lived and worked in the production of the famous aircraft.

Chapter Nine - A Final Flight

After my enforced removal from the world of aviation Industry in 1972 which had sustained and interested me for practically all of my working life and the depressingly hopeless future that seemed to lie ahead, interspersed as it was by so much of hospitals, physiotherapy, increasing immobility which incorporated the now constant daily confinement to the wheelchair, it did not appear unreasonable to assume that my useful life had reached an unsatisfactory conclusion. There is, not unnaturally, a feeling of despair and the frustration in knowing that for the rest of ones days (and nights) even most of the relatively simple facets of living are subject to the assistance of others. There is a form of humiliation in not even being capable of attending to ones basic natural functions without aid that will, unless countered by the affected individual, result in increasing depression and eventually the loss of the will to live.

Fortunately and in this respect I consider myself to have been extremely fortunate, I had been blessed with a very supportive wife who has stuck by me throughout the many changes and vicissitudes that have been an integral part of our married life - far more than my own failings justified - and who richly deserves the dedication that this book carries.

This support, and that from the other members of my family, with the resilient nature that it has always been my good fortune to enjoy, soon cast aside the dark cloud that hovered over the first couple of months when I knew I was never to work for my living again, so the long hours of lying in hospital beds and at home were spent in reading, watching television and by keeping abreast of what was happening in the world outside, my mind kept itself alert, whilst the small amount of grey matter residing unused in my cranium began to stretch itself on the problems of the days as they rolled tirelessly by until gradually certain definite lines of thought caused me to first, write an account of my early days with the Supermarine Aircraft Company and the untold story of the men and women on the factory floor during those heady days before the War burst into all our lives in a way that was to alter it completely for most of us. There had been published many books and articles about the Spitfire and the pre and post war years of the Supermarine Company until its demise in the 1960's, but none so far as I could ascertain, told the story from the particular viewpoint I had held, nor did all their statements of those days align with my personal experiences as an unavoidable participant.

As a means of providing some physiotherapeutic exercise to my badly distorted fingers and hands I began to write (and the dreadful scrawl that resulted has to be seen to be believed) first about the actual air raids on the Woolston and Itchen Works and then, with encouragement from others, the subsequent dispersal that followed the raids, and eventually from those humble beginnings grew the book 'Spitfire Odyssey' which was published in 1985 after being typed into a manuscript by my ex-secretary who found the occupation useful in overcoming the postnatal depression she was experiencing at the time.

Later I learnt to use a typewriter myself with the aid of a rubber ended pencil in lieu of the fingers of my right hand - I am using the same method at this moment - and by this means extended the original manuscript to encompass the whole of my time in the Vickers - Supermarine organisation.

Early in 1984 I wrote to the Head of Documentaries of our local television station to draw their attention to the 1986 anniversary of the prototype Spitfire's first flight with its local interest and connections, and stating that I had a manuscript of original and unpublished material.

The response was swift and effective by a telephone call asking me to meet Peter Williams at the Northam T.V. Centre. We met and talked a short while as he thumbed through the manuscript until he asked if he might read it during a flight he was making to Germany the next day. Naturally concerned for the safety of my precious manuscript I was pleased when he offered to have it photocopied and post the original to me, which he did. There the matter rested for his consideration and for a few weeks nothing more was heard. Then, one afternoon his personal assistant rang me from his Maidstone base office to ask me to watch a T.V. programme being shown one morning about the Spitfire and let them have my comments on it.

I duly watched - it was the Thorn E.M.I. film - and rang back later to say that in my opinion it would be difficult to attempt to improve on that film and not worthwhile to try to go one better on the same basis. I knew it was impracticable to try to make a film of my book because of its being almost beyond the realms of reason to establish even the locations let alone the expensive special effects that would be required to simulate just the air raids. I had almost abandoned hope that anything might come of my initial approach but I had severely underrated the quality of Peter Williams and his researchers.

Somehow they had got wind of a man who had rebuilt a two-seat Spitfire to full flying standard and fortunately had some video film of his own of some of the stages during its constructions. The self imposed task that Nick Grace undertook was of five years duration as he literally built this aircraft from two Pickford vanloads of bits and pieces that he bought from the Strathallan Collection sale in Scotland, transported it down to an airfield in Cornwall and with great patience and skill rebuilt it until it could be flown and pass the Ministry clearances required of any flying machine.

With this as their 'anchor story' the TVS team very cleverly produced their anniversary contribution to the Spitfire celebrations in 1986 entitled 'The Perfect Lady.' They actually wanted to use the title from my book, as in its way Nick Grace's 'Odyssey' was equal to my own, but by then the book was in the throes of publication and we thought that one title might tend to mislead the other. So it became 'The Perfect Lady', something that I am sure most of its pilots would appreciate, and a name that was originally bestowed on it during the War years by Squadron Leader Alan Deere whose adventures in Spitfires during the Air Battles of 1940 and after are another story and lends credence to the title.

The T.V. people were kind enough to slot a small piece in the run-up to the main story for me to have a few words, the filming of which took place 'on location' alongside the River Itchen with the site of the old Woolston Works in the background. After the film was complete they presented me with a copy of the video tape which I still treasure, but it was as a result of this film that I wrote to Nick Grace telling him of my part in instigating the creation of 'his' story and expressing the wish that if it were possible how

The Author on location for the television documentry 'The Perfect Lady' August 2nd 1985. Author.

much I would love to have a flight in his Spitfire. A reply from his charming wife, Carolyn, assured me that if it was possible they would be glad to accommodate me.

Of course then the truth about my disabilities had to come out into the open. There was no way that I could have got myself into that tiny cockpit, neither, so far as I could see, was there much hope in trying to get enough willing, strong, hands to physically deposit me into it, and then get me out again afterwards as the one thing I cannot have is being lifted under the armpits due to the state of my spine at the neck.

For well over a year the matter lay unresolved, the will on all sides undiminished, but the sheer logistics seemingly presenting insoluble problems. It was resolved eventually by a series of lucky coincidences.

My book, 'Spitfire Odyssey', was very well received among the Spitfire 'buffs' and ex-Supermariners in particular and before very long after publication the letters began to arrive from old colleagues with whom I had lost touch and even more surprisingly from persons completely unknown to me who had read the book, enjoyed it, and were kind enough to write and say so. Among the ex-colleagues came one from John Thompson, who in my days post-war with Supermarines had been in the Hursley Planning Office and remembered me from my ratefixing days. He was now Works Manager of the factory at Old Sarum making the new 'Optica' air-craft and suggested that perhaps I might like to visit and have a look round his works? Having explained in a subsequent telephone call my wheelchair reliance and received his assurance that this would be no handicap we went one Saturday morning and I thor-oughly enjoyed the sights, sounds and smells associated with an aircraft factory building a small aircraft whose construction was not all that far removed from the techniques that I had been famil-iar with.

Some months later, when I was cogitating the problem of getting my Spitfire flight, it suddenly came to me that if Nick Grace could come to the Old Sarum airfield when he was in the locality, and if John Thompson could arrange for the use of his fork lift, with a little ingenuity and my slings normally used for hoisting me in and out of bed or bath, it might be possible to sling me over the rear cockpit and lower me in, and by leaving the posterior sling in position during the flight by this means I might be successfully hoisted out. I put the idea to John who sent me post-haste details of the parameters that their forklift operated and what was more important the news that Nick Grace was actually coming to Old Sarum for some event associated with his Insurers! Having checked the performance specifications of the forklift I was certain that it provided an answer to the 'logistics' problem so without more ado I rang Carolyn Grace and explained these fortunate coincidences. She said she would have a word with Nick when he came home (most of Nick's days seem to be occupied with exhibitions and flying displays ever since the Perfect Lady film had brought it to prominence, not to mention the constant maintenance the air-craft required, and the worrisome period he had when the under-carriage failed to lock as he was landing at Eastleigh Airport dur-ing the Spitfire Anniversary display there in March 1986) and next day she phoned to say that providing nothing untoward occurred beforehand, Nick would fit me in at ten o'clock on Saturday, 11th July 1987, before he attended to the business he already had in hand at Old Sarum.

Ready to go in ML 407. Old Sarum airfield. 1987

My wife and I were having one of our rare holiday weeks at a Bourne-mouth Hotel which officially did not end until midday on the 11th July, but as the holiday traffic tends to clog the roads it was decided that we would leave on the Friday night and make the journey from our home to Old Sarum by the back roads so that we would be there in time.

It worked like a charm and we were at Old Sarum by nine-thirty which enabled us to have a dummy run to test the functioning of my slings and John's forklift. It all went very well and just as we finished our testing the sweet noise of a Spitfire's Merlin engine signalled the arrival of the aircraft as it swept low across the airfield prior to banking round to make a landing approach from the eastern end. The old familiar crackle and pop of the taxying Rolls-Royce engine as it headed towards us filled me with memories of those wartime years when it was such a familiar sound in my ears on the High Post airfield barely a couple of miles from where we now stood.

We lost little time in getting down to the main business, just enough to make the formal introductions and then the Spitfire was pushed onto the hardstanding so that the forklift wheels would not sink into the airfield grass with yours truly swinging aloft. I think Nick

Hoisted aloft by forklift for my flight in the Spitfire built by Nick Grace. Nick's face says it all. John Thompson, Works Manager of Optica supervising. Author,

Grace thought it one of the funniest things he had witnessed associated with his 'plane, but nevertheless by removing the rear copckpit hood it became relatively easy (and painless) operation to swing me over suspended in slings underneath the lifting forks of the forklift and lower my awkward bulk into the rear cockpit seat. There was no parachute pack to sit on, just a small cushion, but I was past worrying about safety, this was the dream that I never thought I would ever make reality and if the Fates decreed that we were to crash I had long resolved that if I had to go, then this was the way I would choose.

As my upper sling was removed we tucked the lower one under my bottom so that it did not float free in case it got caught in the control mechanisms, and the rear hood was replaced into its slide runners, and whilst we established that my legs would have to rest free from the rudder pedals as I found I could not operate them satisfactorily Nick belted me in and I asked if I could take the controls when we got aloft. He grinned his agreement and asked what I thought I was going to do? My hope was to use the control column to get the nose up in a shallow climb and by pushing the hand-grip to the right I might execute a slow roll. Nick nodded his understanding and leaving the final closure of my cockpit hood to other aircraft engineers who had gathered round to witness this special aircraft if not the strangely unusual embarking of this aged, crippled passenger, he entered the front cockpit and commenced the preflight routine and starting.

The coughing bark of the Merlin 65 engine starting coupled with the vibrating airframe and the wafted smells of exhaust fumes indicated that we were about to depart. The pneumatic hiss of released brakes, the great circling fan of the propeller snatching at the air for traction, a wave of the hand from the pilot to remove the chocks and we began to roll slowly forward. To my consternation this was to coincide with my rear hood beginning to open. It had not properly locked and shouting to Nick was useless in the engine's roar, so I stuck my hand through the gap and fortunately caught the eye of one of the ground crew who signalled the pilot to stop until the offending catch had been safely secured. Then we were taxying away, the trundling sound of the wheels on the slightly bumpy grass airfield giving the whole procedure the authentic Battle of Britain atmosphere as well as bringing back vividly memories of my first flight in an Avro Tutor trainer aeroplane at Hamble forty-nine years earlier.

By the time we had reached the eastern end takeoff start position I had familiarised myself with the dials that I knew I must use when my turn came to do my slow roll. The rate-of-climb, altimeter and airspeed indicator were all carefully noted - I did not intend to make a cock-up of this opportunity for I knew it would never occur again - and then we swung round facing west and with a roar the Merlin leapt into the life that had brought it such renown, the sudden surge forcing me hard back into my seat. With incredible swiftness we were speeding and bumping our way towards the western boundary, the tail lifted, and I watched the airspeed indicator to see what speed it would be when the wheel rumbling would tell me we were airborne. Fifty, sixty, seventy and then as the eighty came close to the flickering needle we were aloft with the usual slight swing as the rudder compensated for the torque from the racing propeller's grip on the air.

I barely had time to notice the anxious knot of family gathered on the airfield below before we swung northwards over the Woodford valley to the west of High Post where in the morning sunlight I could just make out the little cluster of sheds and tiny hangar where I had spent so many wartime hours assembling the single-seat fighter that had been so vital in those hectic days and in whose twin-seat ancestor I was now fulfilling my own 'impossible dream.'

At 250 knots indicated Nick levelled M.L.407 out at approximately 2000 feet and slowly banked her around as Boscombe Down Airfield passed just to our port side. Snug in the rear cockpit I could appreciate the special feeling that pilot's have for the Spitfire. There is a 'oneness' between man and machine which comes from the 'fit' of the cockpit: almost as if it were tailor made, setting so nicely about the shoulders to give more than the impression that one only had to rest back and gently manipulate the controls to become 'master' of the air. The pattern of the Wiltshire landscape slid beneath us to the accompanying gentle swaying of the aircraft as the varied air densities affected our passage due to our low altitude and the rising ground temperatures changed slowly to accommodate another warm sunny day. With some difficulty I managed to keep some idea of our location relevant to the Old Sarum airfield as Nick Grace slowly brought the nose round until we were lined up to the airfield and approaching from the east. I could hear and sense the increased power being applied and this was confirmed by glancing at the throttle controls which were duplicated in my cockpit.

The nose tilted down and with a whoosh and a road we flashed past our ground party at hangar height and with 300 plus indicated on the 'clock' to pull up in a reasonably steep climb to regain the altitude we had sacrificed for our airfield 'shoot-up.' Up and up once more until the altimeter showed the two to three thousand feet that Nick had determined for his operating height and gently turning on a course similar to the original circuit, but this time when we were at our furthest from the airfield and safely over the empty expanses of Salisbury Plain Nick indicated that I could take over the control column - the intercommunication system between our helmets was not functioning properly - and gently grasping the grip I held the Spitfire straight and level until I was sure Nick knew I had her then with slow but deliberate movements I began to check the effect of my movements on the plane's attitudes.

It is no wonder to me any longer why the R.A.F. pilots who were privileged to fly Spitfires speak so affectionately of them. Light to the touch the control responses were positive and immediate. Slight push forward on the 'stick' and the nose dropped and the horizon crept stealthily above that long cowling snout. Pull it back just as gently and it slipped away again. The rate of climb indicated was barely above level flight so I applied a little right movement and watched as the aircraft banked presenting a fuller view of the landscape passing below. I brought her back to straight and level and gave a nod to Nick that I was OK, received a confirming wave of the hands from him signifying that he was 'hands off' and it was all mine to try my slow roll. Firmly but slowly, I pushed the ring grip over to the right, the wing dropped and we were suspended in the air flying on one side when I found that there was not enough strength in my wasted arm muscles to combat the full force of the airflow on the ailerons. I was aware they were weak but I had hoped they would have coped with that situation until I could have at least taken the Spitfire through the full three hundred and sixty degrees. If ever I cursed this disablement it was then as I realised the fulfilment of my intentions were beyond me and I reversed the stick movement to bring us back to straight and level. Somewhat disappointed and terribly frustrated I waggled the controls to let Nick know that I wanted him to resume full control and once I felt his touch I released my contact.

He must have guessed what had happened: probably sensed the frustration I was suffering, for he lined up again with the airfield and made another low, high speed pass. I waved to my assembled family, then as we hurtled by the nose went sharply up and wonder of wonders, the little plane rolled slowly right through the full circle that I had failed to achieve. For a moment the 'G' forces were applied to my body as never before, my damaged neck felt them and did not like it much, but so far as I was concerned it would have to lump it, I was rolling in a Spitfire, and if I never do anything worthwhile in life again, that for me was a moment of supreme ecstasy. It will remain until my dying day as perhaps the high spot of my life and I would not have missed it for the world.

Nick completed another circuit and then lined the aircraft up to make the landing. The airspeed dropped, the pneumatics hissed as the flaps were lowered and soon there came the familiar 'clunk' as the landing gear went into locked down position. The long nose cowling obscured the forward view - always a complaint about this gem of an aircraft - and slightly fishtailing his way down to see for himself Nick took her gently over the boundary hedge and lowered her with skill and precision on to the grass field cutting back the throttle as soon as possible to shorten the run as the rumbling from the wheels commenced again.

As we taxied back to the group awaiting our return I savoured for a few final moments the experience of the last quarter of an hour. It is beyond my limited means of expression to relate how I felt. Somehow it seemed as though my life had been blessed with this event like an accolade recognising the long association with aircraft and its industry which had been so cruelly shortened and in that respect I would have asked for nothing better, whilst at the same time the youthful hopes that I had entertained at the relevant period to have been the pilot of a fighter aircraft in the world struggle which had interfered with my formative years were revived and in these moments of make-believe the dreams that the youth had formulated then, and carried on into the years that followed, were consummated into a form of reality which eliminated the latent longings that had remained with me prior to this day. I had got it 'out of my system' which is no bad thing.

Nick Grace swung the aircraft on to the hardstanding so that the forklift could operate on a firm base and the reverse procedure to my 'installation' was carried out without mishap and as I swung away the Merlin engine creaked and quietly popped as it cooled down after its stopping whilst the scent of newly cut airfield grass overcame the smell of exhaust fume and hot metal that had enfolded their aroma around me for a short, but unforgettable, fifteen minutes.

What can one say to someone who makes a dream come true, especially when one is still emotionally affected by it and trying hard not to show it. My few gabbled words of thanks to Nick Grace were stumbled over and I hope compensated by the copy of my book that I gave him and the later letter and copies of the photographs that had been taken during my unusual 'installation', and then it was back to the wheelchair to watch some of the subsequent flights that Nick made with his guests. Later a more composed person was able to thank John Thompson for the notable part he had played in making the whole thing possible before we gathered the family together to depart - the Spitfire shooting-up the airfield once again as we did so with yet another passenger. I don't think I was very talkative as we drove home, my thoughts were still 'in the air' where they remained for many a subsequent day.

Sadly I have to relate that some fifteen months later Nick Grace was killed in a road accident - a dreadful loss of a genuinely nice man - but the enthusiasm and spirit that he brought to his endeavours has survived, as his wife Carolyn; determined not to let his magnificent efforts be in vain, took flying lessons herself and then courageously flew solo in Nick's Spitfire. Thankfully, this episode too was captured by our local television station and both 'The Perfect Lady' and 'Carolyn's Flight' are available on a video tape for all to see in a purchasable cassette form.

There has also been a more recent development in the Spitfire saga. The Spitfire Society under the auspices of its founder Group Captain David Green, and inspired by Jeffrey Quill, have had built a full scale replica of the prototype K 5054. Externally it is as accurate in size and detail as it was possible to create, and intended for future generations to see with their eyes, and wonder in their minds, of the artistry and skills of its creator R.J. Mitchell, his design team, and the many who built a thing of such deadly beauty whose history is now enshrined in the period of which we all hope was the last great war.

As will be seen from the photographs it would take a real Spitfire 'buff' to realise that the replica is not quite as the original was on its maiden flight - the modified rudder horn to the fin and the one piece engine cowling side panels that followed after the first flights are evidence of that - but I am certain that every one will agree that it is a worthy memorial to a great aircraft designer and to all who had a share in its successes whether they were on the ground or in the air.

It was particularly appropriate that its unveiling was carried out at its initial display at Hendon's Royal Air Force Museum by Jeffrey Quill who, though in poor health, flew from his Isle of Man home to officiate and see his dream fulfilled.

The latest news of its location that I have is that it is in the Southampton Aviation Museum, but my hope is that one day soon it will be suitably displayed at the Southampton/Eastleigh Airport close to the place where the original made its first flight and so reach full circle.

The beautiful replica of the Spitfire prototype at its build site near Andover. April 1993. Source Tony Spooner.